The Power of Circles

The Power of Circles

A Guide to Building Peaceful, Just, and Productive Communities
—One Circle at a Time

Norman G. Lavery

FOREWORD BY
Mark S. Umbreit

RESOURCE *Publications* · Eugene, Oregon

THE POWER OF CIRCLES
A Guide to Building Peaceful, Just, and Productive Communities
—One Circle at a Time

Resource Publications
An Imprint of Wipf and Stock Publishers
199 W. 8th Ave., Suite 3
Eugene, OR 97401

www.wipfandstock.com

PAPERBACK ISBN: 978-1-4982-8134-8
HARDCOVER ISBN: 978-1-4982-8136-2
EBOOK ISBN: 978-1-4982-8135-5

Manufactured in the U.S.A.

Contents

Foreword

THROUGHOUT THE CENTURIES IN countless cultures the circle process, in one form or another, has been an essential part of building healthy communities, resolving conflicts, and fostering a deep sense of our interconnectedness and yearning for peace. The specific manner in which the circle process is conducted may vary in different settings, but the energy of the circle is most often a constant: a consistent energy that cultivates respect, humility, authenticity, and wisdom.

Norm Lavery in his new book *The Power of Circles* does an unusually good job of describing the full energy and impact of the circle process, moving far beyond just the underlying principles and practices, the core values, the history and indigenous roots, all of which are central to understanding the power, the impact, and what many describe as the magic of the circle process. Few other books so thoroughly move beyond just the techniques and a specific context for the practice of the circle process to describe the wide range of settings in which the power of the circle can be applied.

The Power of Circles is an important addition to the growing literature on the circle process and its many applications. Most importantly, Lavery provides clarity and recognition of where the wisdom of the circle process emerged from and has been practiced as a way of life for centuries among so many of the indigenous people of this planet. Overall, this book you are about to read provides very practical information on how to implement and apply the circle process in multiple settings, followed by helpful guidance on future issues facing the field.

Mark Umbreit, PhD

Center for Restorative Justice & Peacemaking
University of Minnesota
February 2016

Preface

Why This Book Is Being Written

"THIS IS THE FIRST time in my life that anyone has said anything positive about me", sixteen-year-old Sarah whispered through her tears after Circle participants had told her that she is a beautiful person with unlimited potential. This book is for Sarah.

This book is for Chandler, who, having driven the car in which two of his friends had been killed, began to rebuild his life in the supportive Circle environment.

This book is for Julie, who gave me a hug as she stepped down from the stage after receiving her high school diploma.

And this book is for the five young men and their parents who, in a Circle, were able to talk openly about a shoplifting incident and the challenges of being teenagers.

This book is dedicated to all of the individuals and groups who have been helped by the Circle process, and to the many volunteers who have given them the gift of listening and caring.

We honor all indigenous people who, for thousands of years, have understood the importance of Circles, who have used the Circle process in their families and communities every day, and who have kept the power of the Circle process alive in their cultures so that we may benefit from it. The Circle process is a gift, and our responsibility is to use it wisely.

Circles are everywhere in our lives; from the tires we drive on at great speeds, to the bottle caps on our favorite beverages, to the games our children play during recess, and to the silent ripples on our favorite fishing pond. Without the circled wagons of the pioneers, many of us might never have been born; without the wheels on our first bicycle, we might still be learning to keep our balance; and without the hoop in the backyard, we might never have become a high school basketball star. We take Circles for granted because they are so common in our lives. Our indigenous forebears, on the other hand, gave Circles a place of great honor—not only for their spiritual and ceremonial significance, but for their practical value in providing protection, and as a gathering place for passing on the cultural stories necessary for survival.

The journey on the pages that follow begins with a recounting of the historical significance of Circles, and then, building on that rich history, posits Circles as a powerful metaphor and real-life geometry for overcoming some of our culture's deficiencies, and for guiding us toward more fulfilled lives. The journey that unfolds elevates Circles to their just position of eminence, and offers suggestions for their use in families, neighborhoods, and communities of all types and sizes.

As we face the often overwhelming, rapid-paced environment of the twenty-first century, we have an opportunity, using Circles, to build personal and community futures that are both manageable and overflowing with hope and possibilities. We are the travelers on this journey, and the Circle process is our conveyance. Once we understand and embrace the power of the Circle process, we will communicate with each other in much better ways, boldly express our rights as citizens, and work together to build the communities we all desire.

In order to move forward realistically, we must first assess the attitudes and behaviors that define our current culture: conflicts seem to be pervasive in our families, neighborhoods, towns, and businesses; people avoid civic processes because they feel that their words will not be listened to; individuals and groups lack a forum for discussing new ideas and for reaching decisions in a democratic way; and ubiquitous electronic communication tools preclude the face-to-face sharing of stories that in the past ensured the transfer of wisdom to the next generation.

There is hope; there is a better way. And the Circle process is the key.

This book is about Circles: as geometric shapes, symbols, metaphors, containers, and portals; about their occurrence in nature, art, and technology; about their historical significance; and about their power for resolving conflicts, engaging people in civic processes, strengthening relationships, eliciting and building on creative ideas, and celebrating communities in which the full potential of every man, woman, and child is realized. It is a guide for using the Circle process, but above all else it is about the power of Circles and the magic that the Circle process can bring into our lives.

Disclaimer

I am a Caucasian resident of the United States, and have no affiliation with any indigenous clan or tribe. Because the Circle process is so integral to indigenous cultures that are built around clan and tribal units, I struggled for many years with the question of how I could possibly hope to participate in the Circle process in a meaningful and respectful way. After much searching, I finally realized that, with each Circle I convene or of which I am a part, I am helping people experience a sense of connectedness and inclusion in a caring community—the same feeling that is a touchstone of the indigenous Circle processes that we will explore below.

The thoughts and words that follow build on the research and writings of many other people, both in indigenous communities and in non-indigenous cultures, and is not intended to be a definitive treatise on Circle processes or on any other subject. Each time I read a book or a journal article, I am introduced to new resources on the subject of human interactions. This book is offered as a synthesis of my ideas—and those of many other concerned human beings—at this point in time, with a request that each reader build on it to achieve even better ways for all of us to interact.

I have included numerous quotations in the text for two reasons: first, to properly honor the wisdom of previous thinkers and writers, and second, to avoid any possible misinterpretation that might be caused by paraphrasing their words. For those phrases for which no citations are given, I respectfully acknowledge that this book builds on the ideas and words of many of the pioneers in the fields of restorative justice and the Circle process.

Acknowledgments

I ACKNOWLEDGE THE WISDOM of the many individuals who have contributed their insights to me through their writings and through my personal conversations with them. Judge Barry Stuart, through his publications and videos, is an articulate emissary of restorative justice and the Circle process. A recent visit with Barry at his home in Squamish, BC, added greatly to my understanding and appreciation of his role in the development and nurturing of the Circle process. Phillip Gatensby, a Tlingit tribal member with whom I spent a week in a Circle training seminar, continues to be an inspiration through the healing work that he and his brother Harold are doing in the Yukon. I am honored to have spent memorable time with Mark Umbreit, Howard Zehr, and Kay Pranis, all of whom are leaders in the field of restorative justice. And special thanks to Heidi Gjefle, Joan Kresich, and Lorenn Walker, all of whom graciously read early drafts of the manuscript and guided its journey in a good way.

I build on the wisdom I have gained from the above individuals, and on my experiences gained over the past twenty-three years—as a mediator and as the founder of and participant in the Community Circles restorative justice program.

I express gratitude to my parents, to my wife, Marion, and to our daughters, Kristin and Kendra, all of whom have supported me in my passion for exploration, the creative process, and the quest to develop better ways for all of us to interact more effectively.

Introduction

The Journey

This is the story of how we have interacted with each other in the past, and about the potential we have to interact more positively in the future—if we are willing to commit to the hard work of bringing that future to fruition. The foundation for the story is the Circle process—the same Circle process that has guided people to connect with each other for common purposes for thousands of years, and that has allowed people who care about each other to fulfill their shared goal of building healthy lives and communities.

This book is a guide rather than a blueprint—a guide for using the Circle process in a way that fits the culture of *your* family, *your* neighborhood, *your* town, or *your* business group—your own very special community. It is about the potential of the Circle process for building/rebuilding family units, neighborhoods, civic and business organizations.

As we explore the Circle process together, each of us will see and interpret it in the context of our own lives. We will look back at the journeys we have been on and recognize those times when the Circle process could have been helpful, and we will look forward to the next chapter of our lives and visualize how the power of the Circle process can be of value to us personally—to our interactions with relatives and loved ones, and to our social and professional associations. Advances on the ideas presented are expected and welcomed, as you build on them based on your own experience banks.

A Balancing Act

We will balance on the danger/secure ridgeline of the reader's thoughts, feelings, and expectations; and this is done by design. The book is not meant to be a pleasant, cozy read, especially for those people who are now comfortable in professions or lifestyles in which ease and security are guaranteed by the status quo. It is meant to challenge, not console; to provoke rather than provide relaxation. It is about a new yet ancient way of bringing people together and interacting meaningfully. It is about learning to value each of our fellow human beings for their gifts.

Hope and Possibilities

Our focus will be on hope, and hope trumps negativity every time. It is my intent to share my hope with you. In the words of a recent Community Circles participant:

> *Thanks for all your support. You'll never know how much people like you mean to the world. You make my life better.*

The Circle process engages people in the exploration of possibilities, and builds on their innate ability to solve their own problems and design their own positive futures. The Circle process supports them on that journey. It is a way to change the conversation from a focus on problems, failures, shortcomings, and divisiveness to a focus on, and appreciation of, talents, assets, and resources—the gifts that all people have within them.

Communities—Places of Belonging

The Circle process is a uniquely capable tool for building communities. Circles enhance a sense of belonging by providing an incentive for people to participate fully by choice, rather than by obligation. The Circle process engages people and keeps them from lapsing into isolation. The wisdom of all people—including those who are outsiders on the fringes of our society—is a gift we cannot afford to lose. When *all* people are included in the conversation, they develop a caring attitude towards others and become accountable to the group—to their community. The Circle process is inclusive and respectful by design, and is a powerful force for developing vibrant and healthy communities.

The Costs of the Status Quo

The competitive mindset of politicians, other policy makers, and of the American formal legal system (hereafter termed the "formal legal system"), is costly in terms of dollars spent and human potential squandered. Battles often create further problems instead of resolving them, and the punishment paradigm that incarcerates non-violent offenders comes at a great financial cost. Of even greater cost is the loss of the potential contributions of incarcerated individuals to their families and communities. The Circle process is a way to drastically decrease the need for, and the cost of, battles; to decrease the need for punishment; and to achieve positive interactions between people and groups of all types and sizes.

My Concerns

I, like all conscientious citizens, have concerns about the path that our society is on. It will be my intent at all times to present my concerns in a positive frame, as a springboard for dialogue. By building on the good components of our culture rather than engaging in wasteful negativity, it will be my intent to take a small step forward toward achieving more collaborative interactions in communities of all types and sizes. Below are some of my concerns.

I am concerned that our proclivity for, and often reliance on, electronic communication devices is reducing human-to-human contact, increasing our sense of personal isolation, and intensifying our linear, mechanistic view of how to live with each other. Without meeting face-to-face, we have no way to understand each other's needs, desires, and dreams. We have no forum for listening to and building on the creative gifts that each person carries within them. Without rebuilding our interconnectedness as human beings—regardless of gender, race, ethnicity, or religion—we risk becoming even more a world based on competition rather than cooperation, of labeled groups rather than sentient, valued human beings, and of increasingly harsh laws and retribution.

I am concerned with the increasingly contentious attitudes of clients in my mediation practice; the proneness of citizens to engage in legal battles before attempting to resolve differences by talking with one another; the dominance of the argument culture at the local, state, and national levels;

and the inability of groups to communicate in positive ways to achieve their goals—even the goals that they have agreed upon.

I am concerned about people's propensity to apply labels to individuals. Such labeling, e.g., "offender", pigeonholes them, and focuses on their past actions instead of on their potential as human beings.

I am concerned that if we continue to view crimes as offenses against the state rather than as harm caused to individuals, the number of criminals and recidivism rates will increase, and we will have to continue building more prisons and wasting more dollars and lives. The current dominant focus on real or perceived past wrongdoings blocks the energy required to do the creative design work necessary to ensure a positive future.

I am concerned for the future of my children and my grandchildren, and for the lineage yet to be born.

Our Healing Opportunity

Conflicts do not take place between the state and individuals, as in the formal legal system. They occur between human beings and between groups of human beings. In our increasingly technological world, our ability to interact in positive ways is endangered. The Circle process offers a simple and powerful way to reverse this trend, and to repair and enhance relationships. The potential for the Circle process to supplant parts of—or at least to coexist with—current electronic technology, and to thereby improve interactions within families, neighborhoods, and civic and business groups, is compelling.

The Circle process provides a safe place for people to talk about issues of importance to them, with assurance that their words will be listened to. The Circle process focuses on connectedness, human-to-human contact, positive communication patterns, and on the needs and potential of people. It focuses on the future and on healing. Healing rather than punishment is the portal that provides entry to a more peaceful, just, and productive future. When a person in the Sandy Lake Reserve in northwestern Ontario makes a mistake, for example, punishment is not a consideration.

> "We never punished" is the oft-repeated claim. We talked to people instead, showed them the proper way to live, encouraged and aided them. If things finally became completely intolerable, such people might be banished. But we never punished.[1]

1. Ross, *Dancing with a Ghost*, 135.

This book proffers the Circle process as a healing tool to fulfill the potential of individuals and their communities.

The Value of Stories

Stories are the lifeblood of all cultures, and they will be incorporated herein to tie the text to the hearts and minds of readers. As we embark on this journey, I invite you to scribe your own stories, share them with your peers, and pass them on to your children and grandchildren.

The Arena

This book focuses on the use of the Circle process within North America. At times I will, however, mention applications to locations and situations beyond our borders, for the purpose of heralding a broader canvas for the ideas presented. For example, one of my concerns is with the use of power by nations to exert their will on less powerful entities. Another concern is with the depersonalization of international conflict by the use of weapons that preclude seeing the faces, knowing the stories, and understanding the reality of the physical, emotional, and economic damage being inflicted on children, parents, grandparents, and cultures. The potential for the Circle process to improve international group interactions is beyond the scope of the current book, but my hope is that the potential will be apparent, and acted upon.

1

The Tack This Book Takes

WE'LL BEGIN OUR JOURNEY with a focus on Circles themselves. Circles—as geometric shapes and metaphors—have guided us for thousands of years, but have always remained slightly beneath the surface of our consciousness. In the chapters that follow, Circles will be raised to their deserved place of importance, and the details of how the Circle process can be used in many different realms will be explored. The focus, however, will always be on the power of the Circle process itself.

The words that we use are important, so I will define the ones that form the nexus of this work: "community," "justice," "Circles," "peaceful," and "productive." The word "Circle(s)" is capitalized throughout, to acknowledge its central role in the story that unfolds. The next two chapters look at our cultural baggage, and at some of the constraints that have kept us from moving forward in a good way. Options for moving forward are posed, and the best one is highlighted. These chapters are a prologue to our detailed look at Circles and the Circle process.

The geometric form of the Circle, along with its historical importance in the birth of the United States, and its role in indigenous cultures, will provide a foundation for our consideration of ways in which we can use the Circle process today. The mechanics of the Circle process will be presented, and the importance of stories and questions in that process will be emphasized. Indigenous Circle practices in a number of cultures around the world will be described to lend substance to the concept of the Circle process.

The restorative justice movement, and the Circle process as one of its manifestations, will be offered as a proem to our charge of viewing human interactions through a new and more positive lens. The potential positive role of the Circle process in our legal system, families, neighborhoods, schools, workplaces, and civic groups will be presented and supported. The Community Circles restorative justice program, as one of a number of emerging and established community justice initiatives in the United States, will be described; and the opportunity, challenge, and attendant risks of thinking and acting creatively and more positively using the Circle process will be clearly stated. In conclusion, we will consider what success looks like, so that we will know when we have arrived, and can plan a proper celebration.

You are invited to consider the material that is presented as a resource for understanding the salient features of our culture—and how we arrived at our present state. You might also choose to use the information as a platform for a personal exploration of the value of stories and questions in your own life. And the background on indigenous uses of the Circle process might entice you to explore the broad field of anthropology.

All of the ideas presented are intended to be a guide for using the Circle process to serve the culture of your own unique and special community. They comprise a Circles framework for groups of all types and sizes to interact more effectively in the building and maintaining of relationships within peaceful, just, and productive communities.

2
Definitions of Key Terms

THE TERMS "COMMUNITY," "JUSTICE," and "Circles" are mere words when
considered singly. When joined together to create the new terms "community justice," "community Circles," and "justice Circles," a powerful synergy
unfolds. Let's look closely at each of these three key terms, along with the
value terms "peaceful" and "productive."

Community

"Community" is an important word and concept. We hear the word every
day—used in many different contexts. A dictionary definition is: "a group
of people living together in one place, especially one practicing common
ownership; .... a particular area or place considered together with its inhabitants; .... a feeling of fellowship with others as a result of sharing common attitudes, interests, and goals."[1]

The first two definitions refer first to place and then to the inhabitants
thereof. The third definition references shared feelings without regard to
place. In our mobile society, in which two or more generations living in
proximity is often an anomaly, tying the word "community" strictly to a
sense of place is perhaps outdated. Terms such as "community council" and
"community focus group" indeed refer more to common interests than to
interactions between people based only on their geographic location.

Because this book is about people and relationships, I choose to introduce the following definition: "a community is an assemblage of two or more
individuals or groups with similar interests, who care about each other." A
community may comprise people within a family, a neighborhood, a small
town, or a school; it may include friends, fellow workers, or family members who live in distant locations; or it may include individuals bonded by

---

1. *New Oxford American Dictionary.*

3

a philosophy or set of values. Further, a community may comprise political entities such as states or nations that share a valuable resource such as water or arable land. As we proceed, let's see how this definition holds up.

Justice

"Justice" is a word we read about or hear every day. For example:

- With liberty and justice for all.
- If you want peace, work for justice.
- If you want justice, work for peace.
- Distributive justice, retributive justice, restorative justice
- Tribal justice
- Social justice
- Justice court
- Neighborhood justice centers
- The Hague Agenda for Peace and Justice for the 21st Century

A dictionary definition of justice is: "(1) just behavior or treatment; (2) the quality of being fair and reasonable; (3) the administration of the law or authority in maintaining these. Continuing, the definition of "bring someone to justice" is to "arrest someone for a crime and ensure that they are tried in court."[2]

Far from clarifying the concept of justice, these definitions complicate our understanding of this fundamental element of human interaction. For those readers who desire to challenge themselves, and perhaps clarify their understanding of the meaning of justice, I recommend Michael J. Sandel's book *Justice: What's the Right Thing to Do?* Sandel delves into the thoughts and words of Aristotle, Bentham, Mills, Kant, and other moral philosophers, and addresses the implications of justice when applied to the current social issues of abortion, stem cell research, same-sex marriage, and atonement for acts of our predecessors.

The focus of the present treatise is on improving interactions between individuals and between groups, so we will focus our use of the term "justice" on two definitions that impact us on a daily basis: retributive justice,

2. *New Oxford American Dictionary.*

4

as applied in the formal legal system and the courts; and restorative justice, a hallmark of indigenous cultures.

Retributive Justice

As stated by Howard Zehr, in the formal legal system, crime is a violation of the state.[3] Violations create guilt. Justice requires the state to determine blame (guilt) and impose pain (punishment). The central focus is on offenders getting what they deserve.

The formal legal system asks three questions: (1) what laws have been broken?, (2) who did it?, and (3) what punishment do they deserve? Retributive justice is punitive, impersonal, and state-centered. It discourages offender empathy and taking responsibility. It leaves out victims and the community, and does not address their needs. It separates justice from healing.

Restorative Justice

Again, in the words of Howard Zehr, crime is a violation of people and relationships.[4] Violations create obligations. Justice involves victims, offenders, *and* the community. It focuses on victims' needs, offenders' needs, community needs, and offenders' responsibility for repairing harm. Considering the needs of offenders as well as those of victims presents an opportunity to address the root causes of crime. Restorative justice also asks three questions: (1) who has been hurt?, (2) what are their needs?, and (3) whose obligations are these?

The essence of restorative justice is embodied in the words of Judge Barry Stuart, formerly serving in Whitehorse, Yukon; and Kay Pranis, former Restorative Justice Planner for the Minnesota Department of Corrections.

> This is our problem and we want to solve it in a way that we can heal this person and keep harmony in the community. To me, these are the key objectives of any justice system.[5]

---

3. See Zehr, *Little Book of Restorative Justice*.
4. Ibid.
5. Stuart, in the video *Circle Sentencing: A Yukon Justice Experiment*.

> The very concept of justice calls for inclusion, equal voice, and decisions representing all interests.[6]

Restorative justice, as embodied in the above definitions, is the overarching set of values and principles within which the Circle process resides. It is not a panacea, or necessarily a replacement for the formal legal system. Most restorative justice advocates agree that crime has a societal dimension as well as a more local and personal one—e.g., a teenager who has broken a law but is not a bad person. By putting the spotlight on and elevating the personal dimensions of crime, restorative justice seeks to provide a better balance in how we experience justice.

Restorative justice promotes engagement of all parties affected by crime: victims, offenders, and the community. It is not a particular blueprint. Various programs embody restorative justice principles in part or in full. It is not a map, but it can be viewed as an invitation for exploration.

Circles

A Circle is "a round plane figure whose boundary (the circumference) consists of points equidistant from a fixed point (the center); . . . A group of people with a shared profession, interests, or acquaintances."[7] A common phrase, "the discussion went round and round in Circles," highlights the difference between the linear thought process that pervades our results-oriented culture, and the Circle process, which focuses on relationships, and in which conclusions are not necessarily the *only* goal of human interactions.

The metaphor of a Circle as the boundary of a container works well when considering frontier defensive maneuvers such as circling the wagons, and when viewing a Circle as a perimeter of safety for discussions of important and sometimes sensitive matters. The metaphor is also meaningful when considering Circles as places of gathering, and it is this image that will appear repeatedly in the ensuing discussions of relationships and communities.

Let's delve briefly into the seemingly disparate realms of mathematics and art. If a Circle is cut into wedges, as the number of wedges increases to infinity, a rectangle results[8]; so, although we are focusing on the Circle

---

6. Pranis, "Building Justice."
7. *New Oxford American Dictionary.*
8. Weisstein, *CRC Concise Encyclopedia of Mathematics*, 421.

shape because of its historical and cultural significance, other shapes can provide equally safe boundaries. Let's look at an example.

I was fortunate to have the opportunity to visit the museum housing the Peggy Guggenheim Collection of contemporary art in Venice, Italy. Among the many sculptures, paintings, and constructions by well-known artists, I was stopped speechless by two paintings that were exhibited next to each other. *The Room*, by William Baziotes, and *Personage*, by Robert Motherwell, are both colorful, abstract paintings consisting of overlapping, distorted geometric shapes. (The paintings can be viewed in the catalgue of the Peggy Guggenheim Venice Collection.) I stood motionless for ten minutes, and returned later in the day to again be in their presence, trying to comprehend why they spoke so strongly to me.

You might be buoyed, or possibly repelled, by the two rectangular abstract pieces; or you might give a hearty "so what"—and that's okay. What struck me about the two works, and what continues to resonate, is the seemingly chaotic forms in the paintings—all contained securely within the borders of the canvases. Tying the above observations to the Circle process, many Circle processes are convened because there is some amount of chaos present—in families, neighborhoods, tribes, or other communities— and all of the processes provide a safe and secure container—regardless of the shape of that container. Circle processes around the world differ in how they provide a container for chaos, and some of the processes that are well documented will be described in a later chapter. It is important for me to clarify at this point that not *all* Circle processes involve chaos, with many Circles being convened to support friends, share ideas, or to celebrate good news or life milestones.

Many of the Circles convened in the Community Circles program do involve chaos—revolving around personal relationships, negative activities spurred by peer pressures, lack of compliance with the burdens of multiple court and treatment program mandates, the challenges of living in an adult world without having been given any training for doing so, disagreements among neighbors or business associates, and balancing the needs and responsibilities within the school system. Community Circles supports participants by providing a safe space in which they can talk about issues of importance to them, figure them out, and gain strength in their lives by resolving them. We, as Circle Keepers (the term we use for our trained volunteers), listen, offer guidance from our own life experiences, and securely hold the edges of the canvas so that chaos can be reworked into a meaningful and productive pattern.

Peaceful and Productive

These words capture the qualities of a community that entice people to voluntarily engage with and care for each other. A peaceful and productive community is one in which people are treated with respect, citizens work together to resolve difficulties, and people help others—including those on the fringes—to achieve their full potential. It is a place that focuses on the assets of its participants, on possibilities for the future, and on hope.

3
Where Are We?

WE FACE FOUR MAIN challenges if we are to achieve our potential as individuals and as communities: (1) lack of a forum for discussing limited resources (and their commonly inequitable distribution) and competing societal needs and desires; (2) the baggage of our criticism- and labeling-prone, competitive, fear-based, and quick-fix culture; (3) the constraints of the formal legal system; and (4) our propensity to engage in wasteful argumentation.

Although the depth of the discussion below might appear to some readers to be a profligate use of words and space, it is critical for us to clearly understand the major factors within our culture that are having a negative impact on our ability to interact effectively. The counterpoint, for those who have not yet discerned it, is the power of the Circle process.

Lack of a Forum for Discussing Limited Resources and Competing Societal Needs and Desires

It is commonly assumed that all conflicts are caused by limited resources, or by jousting between competing societal needs and desires. Conflicts, however, are *also* caused by the lack of a meaningful forum in which to discuss resources, needs, and desires.

Consider the frequently utilized public hearing process for offering citizens a voice on a particular issue. One person holds forth, while those in the queue practice their words so when their allotted three minutes arrive they will shine and carry the day. Are the people who are waiting for their turn actually listening to the words of the speaker? Is anyone listening to them? Truly, public hearings have little to do with listening.

The following quotations highlight the importance of listening, in both public and private forums:

People do not listen with the intent to understand; they listen with the intent to reply.[1]

Most conversations are simply monologues delivered in the presence of a witness.[2]

The first duty of love is to listen.[3]

Consider organizations in which one person dictates the behavior required of others, or in which subordinates are allowed to speak but decisions are made only at the top. The "Solomon Trap"[4] refers to a process in which (1) the person responsible for making a decision seeks to identify all affected parties, and asks them for their views; (2) the official sifts through the comments, and crafts a solution that comes nearest to addressing everyone's interests; (3) the decision is announced to the affected parties, who are dismayed that their key issues have not been addressed exactly as they wanted them to be; and (4) the official spends an inordinate amount of time defending the virtues of his or her proposal—at which point the parties are so frustrated and angry that they will not fully support the proposal no matter what accommodations have been made.

Any format that precludes meaningful participation by the individuals impacted by decisions tends to alienate them—an alienation to which I can attest, based on my past career with a major corporation. In the above civic and organizational situations, what is missing is a democratic forum for talking and listening—the key link in preventing conflict, managing conflict, resolving conflict, and getting things done. Our dominant top-down decision-making culture *does* provide someone to take the blame when things go wrong. It also, however, places those people who are below—workers or citizens— in the passive position of waiting for someone to bring light out of darkness and to make decisions for them. The top-down model fails to acknowledge the leadership, accountability, caring, and creative potential of each and every person in a community, including those individuals considered to be living on the fringes. The Circle process provides a forum for listening to and valuing *all* voices in a community, and uses *all* of a community's energy for solving problems and designing a good future.

1. Covey, 7 *Habits of Highly Effective People*, 239.
2. Millar, *Weak-Eyed Bat*, 117.
3. Paul Tillich, http://www.brainyquote.com/quotes/quotes/p/paultillic114351.html.
4. Carpenter and Kennedy, *Managing Public Disputes*, 22.

Our Cultural Baggage

Our Criticism-Prone Culture

We seem to feel an obligation in our culture to come to judgments about things, and to express those judgments at every available opportunity. When asked for an opinion, it is a Western cultural norm to respond, to provide an answer, to state a position, or to render a judgment based on a self-perceived expertise, experience, or view of the world at that particular moment. Positional debate yields a winner and a loser, but it also precludes the opportunity to learn anything of value from the other party.

The term "agonism" derives from the Greek word for a contest or an automatic warlike stance. Deborah Tannen defines agonism as a kind of programmed contentiousness—a pre-patterned, unthinking use of fighting to accomplish goals that do not necessarily require it.[5] The agonistic or knee-jerk use of critical words—without a clear consideration of their potential for harm—is a serious, though frequent, mistake. Polarization of issues, damaged relationships, and senseless expenditure of energy on argumentation are common results.

Our United States culture seems to thrive on criticism, and criticism is truly the haven of mediocre minds. Consider left- or right-biased talk radio or TV programs, or witness the daily political shenanigans in Washington, DC. Criticism is easy, and makes the critic feel superior. It is easy because it is always possible to compare what one sees to a model of one's own choosing. For example, one of the handcrafted wooden rocking chairs that I have designed and produced could be criticized for being simplistic and unimaginative, or the same chair could be criticized for being overly ornate and complex. The individuals making the critiques consider both of their viewpoints to be valid, but neither viewpoint advances a higher purpose of creating a better chair design. Criticism is rampant in family, neighborhood, civic, business, and government groups. Criticism is anathema to the resolution of problems. It stultifies creativity, and it can be devastating to individuals' esteem. Broadening the context to discussions between states and between nations, such exchanges are also, in large part, couched in negative terms that lead to the use of criticism to justify acts of suppression and aggression.

5. Tannen, *Argument Culture*, 8.

Indigenous cultures in northern Ontario take a much different approach to the issue of criticism. It is considered wrong to give advice, even when it is asked for. In the words of Dr. Clare Brant:

> The Ethic of Non-Interference is probably one of the oldest and one of the most pervasive of all the ethics by which we Native people live. It has been practiced for twenty-five or thirty thousand years, but it is not very well articulated. . . . This principle essentially means that an Indian will never interfere in any way with the rights, privileges and activities of another person. . . . This principle of non-interference is all pervasive throughout our entire culture. *We are very loath to confront people. We are very loath to give advice to anyone if the person is not specifically asking for advice. To interfere or even comment on their behavior is considered rude.*[6]

> Anything which might cause another person to lose face, to feel inadequate, foolish, or stupid, would be a blow to that self-esteem and an impediment to their development as a human being.[7]

> A multitude of studies point to self-esteem problems as an important source of violence, especially against women and children. The denigration and abuse of others—the demonstration of power over them—is in large part a desperate assertion of self. . . . The Elders seem to think it counter-productive to tell an offender constantly how much damage he has done, how he has hurt others, how it is his failure to control his harmful impulses that is to blame. Instead, they seem to make a deliberate attempt to improve each offender's self-esteem by reminding him of his potential for goodness, of his capacity to move forward, with help, towards self-fulfillment. Their constant emphasis is upon respect, *including respect for one's self.* . . . We can also see why the Elders favour the use of instructive parables over direct criticism. Criticism focuses almost entirely upon the past, and upon failures in that past, while enlightening parables instead serve to coax people forward towards better ways of doing things in the future.[8]

The Circle process is non-judgmental, and builds *only* on positive ideas forwarded by participants.

---

6. Ross, *Dancing with a Ghost*, 12–13.

7. Ibid., 24.

8. Ibid., 172–73.

Our Penchant for Value-Laden, Judgmental Labels

Labels are an important component of interpersonal communication, although we are seldom aware of them. They help to accurately transfer information, express ideas and describe feelings, sometimes simplify complex situations, and provide much of the nuance that makes the English language both colorful and vibrant.

Some labels are non-judgmental and have no value implications—e.g., "There goes a purple bus with chrome wheels and yellow lights all around the top. It's painted to look like a dinosaur." Other labels are judgmental and laden with value connotations. The use of labels in this way is an accepted strategy in product advertising—e.g., "Designer jeans will improve your self-esteem as well as your figure." Use of the label "glamorous" in tobacco advertising implies that people who do *not* use tobacco are not glamorous.

We hear value-laden, judgmental labels every day—e.g., "That teenager is dressed like a slob. Just look at the gaudy tattoos, metal chains, body piercings, and mobster pants. No doubt he's a loser and is guilty of dealing drugs."

Judgmental labeling is a tenet of the formal legal system. The judgmental label "offender," which we read daily in the newspaper, doesn't tell us much about whether the recipient is deserving of the brand, but only about the writer's personal conclusion. The label of "offender" freezes a person permanently in time. A court-determined "felon" is a felon for life—with no consideration of his or her capability for positive change. Value-laden, judgmental labels rank people as being either better or worse, get in the way of increasing our knowledge of them, and limit our capacity to think in intelligent and objective ways.

When value-laden, judgmental labels are used to drive wedges between people—to willfully cause harm, to obfuscate truth, or to foment competitive and destructive attitudes and behaviors—their use is wrong. When people use value-laden terms such as "toxic," "dangerous," "high level," "polluting," and "poisonous"—without accurately and clearly defining them—they are doing so for some purpose other than that of transmitting information truthfully, and they should be held accountable. Judgmental labeling also has a negative impact within families (such as verbal and emotional abuse between spouses, parents, and children), in schools (bullying); communities (rancorous debate on public issues), and in workplaces (workers isolated within the organization). When value-laden, judgmental statements are used, they exhibit certainty, and exclude the possibility that things might be different from the way the speaker perceives them or that other people might have a different yet equally valid perception. Such labels polarize people and open the door for conflict to enter, because we can be assured that not everyone will agree with us.

An Ojibway woman spoke at a workshop on sexual abuse of children:

> She indicated that she wanted to speak in Ojibway, not in English, for two reasons. First, she wanted to be certain that the Elders who were present would be able to understand what she said. The second reason, however, was more fundamental than that. As she described it, Ojibway was a "softer" language than English when it came to describing such things. Ojibway did not contain expressions for such concepts as "the accused" or "the offender," concepts which have the effect of stigmatizing the person involved. Ojibway terms, she told me, would not amount to "labels" like our words would, for they would not characterize the person but describe, in gentle terms, what he or she had done. They are verb-oriented expressions, not categorizing nouns, and as such they do not "freeze" a person within a particular classification for the rest of his life. With their emphasis on activity, these words instead emphasize process rather than state, thus helping the person who hears them to understand that all of life is a process and every person is a "thing-which-is-becoming," as opposed to a "thing-which-is." From this perspective, no one can be written off because of what they did at a particular moment in time. Instead, since each person is always "someone-in-the-making," it becomes everyone's duty to assist in the process.[9]

The Circle process provides time and space for supporting the integrity of all individuals.

Our Competitive Culture

I am grateful to Tannen[10] and Ross[11] for the framework within which the information below is presented. Competition is an American cultural addiction. Competition is not so much about scarce resources as it is a cultural norm. From the young age at which we win gold stars for spelling bees, to our teens when we treasure sports trophies, to the exhilaration

9. Ibid., 163–64.
10. Tannen, *Argument Culture.*
11. Ross, *Dancing with a Ghost,* and *Returning to the Teachings.*

of beating opponents in high school and college debates, to having our children rank in the 98th percentile in height and weight development, to the ascension to the corner office in corporate headquarters—competition rules. Even in our senior years, prizes are awarded for beating our friends at bridge, pinochle, and bingo. We are constantly being ranked in comparison to other individuals. It is this mania for competition that defines the win-lose framework within which we educate our children, raise our families, pursue our careers, and attempt to resolve our differences. I am better than you are; only one of us can win; my success means that you will fail.

Sport is a common metaphor for competition. For many children, competitive sports operate as a failure factory that not only effectively eliminates the "bad ones," but also turns off many of the "good ones."

> A personality profile administered to fifteen thousand athletes re-
> vealed "low interest in receiving support and concern from others,
> low need to take care of others, and low need for affiliation. Such a
> personality, the researchers conclude, seems necessary to achieve
> victory over others."[12]

War is the ultimate metaphor for competition. It has the greatest opportunity to determine winners and losers (by use of force), to rank nations or ethnic groups as more or less powerful, to destroy property, and to devastate lives and relationships. In the context of his military background, President Eisenhower tied the competitive sports metaphor to that of the battlefield when he said:

> "the true mission of American sports is to prepare young people
> for war."[13]

The formal legal system is predicated on battlefield tactics. It is an adversarial system in which lawyers have an ethical obligation to fight for their clients.

> Monroe Freedman, former dean and professor of legal ethics at
> Hofstra University Law School, quotes sources from as far back
> as the 1908 Canons of Professional Ethics that require a lawyer
> to give "entire devotion to the interests of the client [and] warm
> zeal in the maintenance and defense of his rights," . . . But from
> the point of view of society at large, many now question the eth-
> ics of the adversary system in general and the principle of zealous

12. Kohn, *No Contest*, 134.
13. Quoted in ibid., 145.

advocacy in particular—because it often serves to obscure the truth rather than reveal it, because it is inhumane to the victims of cross-examination, and because of what it does to those who practice within the system, requiring them to put aside their consciences and natural inclination toward human compassion.[14]

We live in an age in which computers code information with zeros and ones. No other choices are possible. Our culture is similarly constrained by either/or oppositional thinking, with examples being the labels of good/bad, right/wrong, success/failure, white/black, truth/falsehood, gifted/not gifted, and winner/loser. There is no reason that choices *have to be* presented in twos, but arguments, oppositional viewpoints, and debates *do* sell print media and television advertising and *do* elect political candidates. In competitive environments, people talk at or about other people, but seldom with them.

Rupert Ross and Petr Kropotkin state clearly that competition is *not* an appropriate or effective model of interaction in indigenous cultures and in the animal kingdom:

> We seem to reward victors almost regardless of *how* they won, and at times life seems defined as a series of activities specifically created just to separate winners from losers. . . . This law of fierce competition, however, does not appear to be the law that many Aboriginal peoples derive from their study of the nonhuman world. Instead, they have drawn an opposite conclusion: that Creation demonstrates, at its most fundamental levels, principles of mutualism, interdependence, and symbiosis. At those levels, all aspects of the created order are essential to the continued survival of Creation as a whole. According to that perspective, the obligation of humans is not to attack, insult, or diminish them or each other, but to demonstrate respect, to offer support, to work towards cooperation.
>
> In this view, even verbal insult is arrogant and wrong, whether the target is other humans, animals, plants, or Earth.[15]

> The first thing which strikes us as soon as we begin studying the struggle for existence under both its aspects—direct and metaphorical—is the abundance of facts of mutual aid, not only for rearing progeny, as recognized by most evolutionists, but also for the safety of the individual, and for providing it with the necessary

14. Tannen, *Argment Culture*, 145–46.
15. Ross, *Returning to the Teachings*, 77–78.

food. With many large divisions of the animal kingdom mutual aid is the rule.[16]

The result appears to be that Western science has achieved special excellence in its understanding of things and their properties, while Aboriginal science has achieved a special excellence, only now being recognized, in how things work together within systems-as-a-whole. In fact . . . Western scientists have recently "granted" Aboriginal science its own acronym, TEK, which stands for Traditional Ecological Knowledge.

This determination to place the primary emphasis on studying the relationship between things—and to try to accommodate those relationships instead of dominating the things within them—seems to lie at the heart of a great many Aboriginal approaches to life.[17]

What if we defined our lives not as occupying the new ground of our own discoveries but as revisiting ground already occupied by all our ancestors? Our predominant sense of self would be largely shaped by the conviction that we were going where others had gone before and where others would always go. We would be taking our turn at the wheel of life rather than moving ahead from where others had left off. The shape of existence would be circular, not evolving, but *revolving*. The past, present and future would always be essentially the same. Just as the four seasons come, go, and always return again, so too each generation would come and go, never striking out on its own path. Instead, it would retrace the path of the last. Each generation's turn at the wheel might include performances better or worse than those of the last, but they would be essentially the same performances, with the same set and script and plotting. . . .

There may be a synergy of sorts here: the more we cover new ground, the more we feel unconnected to either a familiar past or future, then the more we may also feel a pressing need to leave our mark by building or exploring something new. By going further, faster or higher than anyone has gone before, we may merely be wishing to find some way to erect a sign that says "I was here."

But if, by contrast, we did not think that we travelled a new road alone but an old road worn smooth by our ancestors, would we not be less concerned with such testaments to our presence?

16. Kropotkin, *Mutual Aid*, 9–10.
17. Ross, *Returning to the Teachings*, 63.

Would we have the same preoccupation with what is new, with leaving our singular mark for all to see? Or would we instead find our sense of continuity in the fact that our descendants would not have to "look back" to know of us, for they would be walking on our trails. . . . The only imperative, then, would involve not leaving a monument but instead an undefiled terrain, as suitable for their use as it was for ours.[18]

The non-competitive Circle process, with its documented successes over thousands of years in indigenous cultures, counters all that is destructive in the competitive process that pervades Western culture.

Our Fear-Based Culture

The marketing of fear supports the *perceived* need for greater leadership control, more laws, and more restraint of wrongdoers and of individuals on the fringes of society. The retributive agenda gets packaged as spiritual values, family values (and variations thereof), the American way, and love it or lose it—all under the umbrella of a need for greater funds for law enforcement. Nightly TV news broadcasts highlight law-breaking incidents in our communities and support the perceived need for more taxpayer attention to issues of law, order, and incarceration. Marketing of fault fuels our belief that if we can assign blame and enact punishment then our problems will be solved and will not happen again. It is a response to a perceived need to take action—or rather to have police officers take action—rather than a response of committing community energy to finding durable answers to complex problems. It also is a subtle argument against diversity and inclusion. The belief that we can solve all community problems with stricter rules and more taxpayer dollars is false.

The marketing of fear linked to those individuals who live on the fringes of society is repugnant. The belief that we can resolve issues of poverty, homelessness, mental illness, and addiction by spending more money on one-time treatment programs, and by warehousing non-dangerous people in jails, is not only false, but wasteful of human potential. It is time for us to embrace the reality that the better future we all desire can only be achieved by energizing citizens to create communities in which safety situations rarely arise, and in which people on the fringes are brought into the community and not warehoused on its margins.

18. Ross, *Dancing with a Ghost*, 90–91.

The Circle process is a way for citizens to resolve many contentious situations themselves and, by so doing, allow law enforcement personnel to spend taxpayer resources more effectively in handling the serious criminal and safety issues that they were hired to address. The Circle process provides a forum in which citizens can discuss and resolve community problems; in which they can discuss their needs, desires, and dreams; and in which they can support each other.

Our Quick-Fix Culture

We seem to feel a need to solve problems quickly—instead of embracing a willingness to dedicate time to developing durable, long-term solutions. Durable solutions might require numerous meetings, tolerating people with ideas different from our own, looping discussions back onto previously rejected ideas, talking about relationships, and working in a distinctly non-linear, non-competitive, non-argumentative format. Until we commit to supporting such a philosophy and arrangement, we stand to remain mired in contentious, nonproductive bogs, with citizens choosing nonparticipation over participation because they feel that their voices will not be listened to.

The Circle process ensures that all people can offer their ideas; express their needs, desires, and dreams without criticism; and have confidence that their voices will be listened to. It is a democratic process that has a proven record for achieving durable solutions to community problems.

The Constraints of the Formal Legal System

We are a nation of laws, but our reliance on the "law" to resolve all difficulties robs citizens of their right to resolve many of their own community problems, and diminishes their ability and desire to do so. The law—the formal legal system—is often of great value in dealing with criminal activity and issues of public safety, but its rigidly structured application to non-safety-related infractions is wasteful of manpower, dollars, and lives.

The value of debate in the formal legal system, as an effective tool for determining truth, is moot. The argument premise not only uses inordinate amounts of time, energy, and dollars; it also precludes the emergence of creative ideas that could foretell new and better ways for people to interact with each other in communities of all types and sizes. Incarceration, as an act of punishment for non-violent offenders, is counterproductive. Rather than the healing approach taken by many indigenous cultures, Western incarceration robs society of the gifts that jailed people have to offer and, upon release, casts them back into society with a spitefulness that only increases their probability of reoffending.

Ross, based on his extensive experience working with indigenous groups in Canada, states:

> The function of traditional Native dispute-resolution systems was the real resolution of disputes. They hoped that at the end of their process the parties would be returned to cooperative co-existence, to real interpersonal harmony. Naturally they expected that our courts would have the same goal. Little did they know that we do not even pretend to that goal. Our society is a society of strangers. Our judicial processes do not aim at restoring friendship or harmony, if only because between strangers these qualities do not exist in the first place. Instead, we aim at deterring harmful *activity* so that each stranger can continue to follow his private path without interference. . . . our courts focus primarily on the preservation of public peace. They are concerned not with what people are, but with what they do. The Native approach essentially ignores what was done and concentrates instead on the personal or interpersonal dysfunctions which caused the problem in the first place. Their first priority lies in trying to correct those dysfunctions rather than in trying to keep those continuing dysfunctions from erupting into further harmful or illegal acts.[19]

> Probably one of the most serious gaps in the system is the different perception of wrongdoing and how to treat it. In the non-Native society, committing a crime seems to mean that the individual is a bad person and must be punished. . . . The Indian communities view wrongdoing as a misbehaviour which requires teaching, or an illness which requires healing.[20]

The Circle process provides time and space for people to work together to understand and correct the dysfunctions that lead to the breaking of laws and community expectations.

19. Ibid., 45–46.
20. Ibid., 62.

The Wastefulness of Argumentation

We waste valuable energy engaged in arguments that do little to resolve community issues and that leave scarce time for using people's innate talents to design a more positive future. The argument stratagem negatively affects groups of all types and sizes.

Discernment refers to the differences between objects, groups, and ideas; and discussing those differences leads to learning, understanding, and compassion. Judgment ranks entities on a scale of better or worse, and argumentation based on judgment leads to divisiveness, intolerance, and violence. We, as a culture, spend an inordinate amount of time and energy in judgmental argumentation, with examples of divisive issues being: ethnic characteristics, religious beliefs, educational backgrounds, financial positions, and political viewpoints. Consider the media personalities who define themselves solely in opposition to and better than other individuals, philosophies, and ideas. Time spent in such pursuits is asinine, freshmanic, and destructive, and must be identified as such. Again, such negative behavior is the haven of entrenched and unenlightened minds. The goal of achieving dominance over others will not lead to the development of new and better ideas.

The issues we face as families, neighborhoods, and civic communities are too important to continue with the dedication of time and energy to winning battles—instead of solving problems and designing new and better possibilities. The Circle process offers a powerful way forward.

Summary

Providing a forum in which people can share their ideas, needs, desires, and dreams is crucial to the development of peaceful, just, and productive communities. Dedicating time to listening intently, discerning rather than judging, and building on the positive ideas brought forward by others can bring light into group processes, and can buoy participants with the understanding that each person's views are respected and valued and that each person can make a difference. Developing a positive community attitude toward handling many of its own issues can be a powerful bonding process, and can lead in a very positive way toward healthier community interactions. The Circle process, applicable within communities of all types and sizes, is a proven way in which to overcome the roadblocks listed above.

4

How Did We Get Here?

We'll approach this subject from two vantages. First we'll consider the emergence of the formal legal system in the United States, and then we'll examine the dominant thinking process in our culture.

The Emergence of the American Formal Legal System

The decision-making pattern of indigenous people around the world is the basis for the Circle process presented in this book, and will be discussed in detail in a later chapter. For now, let's focus our attention on what has taken place in the United States since the arrival of white men.

Jerold Auerbach has tracked the development of the formal legal system and alternatives to it.[1] A number of religious common-interest communities were established in the northeastern United States in the 1600s. Dedham, Massachusetts, was a theological community built on "Christian love and harmony," tolerating within its midst only those who were of "one heart with us." Mediation was used to resolve conflicts, members who disagreed with the leaders were expelled, and often a schism resulted in the formation of a new and separate community. Dedham blended church and civilian authority and lasted for fifty years. The Quakers in Pennsylvania were a holy community whose aversion to litigation expressed their commitment to "love, order, and unity of brethren." Early New England towns, bound by common religious ideologies in which survival was a key concern, considered conflict to be disruptive and dangerous. Yet the closeness required by shared living space and common values heightened the intensity of conflicts. Mediation was often used to urge disputants to live together in a way of neighborly love. The absence of judicial activity in many towns suggests that most disputes were resolved through non-legal channels, or

1. Auerbach, *Justice without Law?*

were not permitted to surface because of the religious strictures in place. For the good of the community, conflicts were often suppressed rather than resolved. The litigation process produced feelings subversive to the very purpose for which the above religious communities were created, and so was avoided whenever possible.

> Lay and church leaders in Boston shared a strong bias against lawyers, whom John Cotton denounced as "unconscionable Advocates [who] use their tongues as weapons of unrighteousness . . . to plead to corrupt Causes."[2]

Sharing a suspicion of law and lawyers, religious common-interest communities developed patterns of conflict resolution that reflected their striving for social harmony beyond individual conflict—"justice without law." They believed that where a sense of community ended, the law began.

Some early common-interest communities were based on land ownership or other economic interests. Sudbury, Massachusetts, was an open farming community, with 90 percent of the land owned and worked by settlers for communal benefit. Conflicts were settled by discussion or arbitration. The Sudbury community lasted for twenty years. New Netherland, established by Dutch ruling elite, was designed to capitalize on mercantile opportunities in the New World.

> So the Dutch leaders, concerned with the spread of litigation "to the prejudice and injury of this place and the good people thereof," established an arbitration Board of Nine Men. Rotating panels of "good men," drawn from the upper stratum of Dutch society, exerted strong pressure for reconciliation.[3]

By the end of the seventeenth century, trade between communities along the eastern coast of the United States and with Europe was well developed and, in this commercial environment, the opportunities for individual gain were plentiful. As members of common-interest religious or land-based communities began interacting with outsiders for commercial purposes and private gain, courts replaced churches as dispute resolution forums. With common moral codes supplanted by individual goals, courts became the only institutions whose rules and decisions could gain common acceptance. Law encouraged contentiousness, while channeling it.

2. Ibid., 27.
3. Ibid., 31.

The role of Plymouth, Massachusetts, as the commercial center of the country may have encouraged the tendency of inhabitants to litigate. By glorifying individual gain, commercial values contributed additional centrifugal force to a community already fragmented by individualism and sectarianism.

> In a setting that encouraged economic opportunity and religious dissent, the diminished authority of town, church, and neighbors left a vacuum for law to fill. No longer was conflict suppressed for the common weal; indeed, the meaning of the common weal was unclear. Consequently dispute-settlement procedures, once designed to turn townsmen and parishioners toward each other and inward to their community and congregation, now merely designated winners and losers among competing individuals. Arbitration and mediation had been appropriate for neighbors and parishioners, but the disagreements of strangers, who lacked any basis for mutual trust, were for lawyers and judges to resolve.[4]

The pursuit of self-interest and profit generated its own communitarian values, which commercial arbitration expressed. The competitive individualism of the marketplace was checked by the need for continuing harmonious relations among men who did business with each other. Businessman developed a community of work and profit, as opposed to one of place or prayer. By the mid-eighteenth century, many merchants continued to favor commercial arbitration instead of the courts for its speed and low cost. Not only did courts dispense expensive, endless law, according to one New York merchant, they were slow to develop legal doctrine that facilitated commercial development.

> The quality of a shipment of flour or herring, like the appropriate compensation for salvaging a wrecked ship, was best determined by partners in trade and commerce. . . . Merchants preferred informed business experts, sympathetic to commercial imperatives, to inscrutable judges or ignorant juries. . . . Merchants often valued their commercial relationships (and their profits) over the assertion of legal rights.[5]

Some common-interest communities based on religious beliefs and economic interests that exist today in the United States include the Quakers, Amish, Mennonites, the Amana Colony, and the Maytag Colony. It's

---

4. Ibid., 41.
5. Ibid., 33.

important to note that in these communities, because conflict is considered threatening to group harmony, it is settled internally by elders—by a panel of "understanding men" or by several "judicious" men. Justice without lawyers also continues today to have strong appeal in Scandinavian ethnic communities in North Dakota and Minnesota, where conciliation is a part of their cultural heritage.

The conflict between cultural mores inherited from countries of emigration and the formal legal system in the United States caused both bonding and disquiet within immigrant groups.

> During the early years of the twentieth century, millions of new immigrants to the United States struggled to survive in an alien, often hostile, environment. . . . they settled in neighborhoods where they drew sustenance from others who not only shared the wrenching experience of their passage but the comforting memories of their traditions. . . . Control over conflict was crucial for preserving communal values from the corrosive effects of assimilation. . . . Beyond the mundane conflicts of daily existence were sharp religious and political disputes whose sources lay beyond the ocean in their lands of origin. . . . There was a strong pull toward the legal system. Courts and police were as important as instruments of socialization for adults as schools and teachers were for children. . . . The more closely they conformed to the values of the dominant society the less alien they felt, and the less hostility they were likely to encounter.[6]

The most tenacious defense of traditional practices in the New World came from Chinese and Jewish immigrants. Mediation continues to be an enduring form of conflict resolution in Chinese communities in a number of large cities in the United States. The assertion of rights not only is disruptive; it dangerously elevates the individual above his family, clan, or village. Not only is litigation expensive, time consuming, and unpredictable; it disrupts harmony and represents a degrading confession of personal failure.

> "Once go to law," according to a Chinese admonition, "and there is nothing but trouble."[7]

The retention of disputes within the Jewish community was not merely a defensive response to external hostility. It expressed deep desires for religious and cultural autonomy in exile. The Bet Din, or Rabbinical

6. Ibid., 69–72.
7. Ibid., 74.

Court, was in theory restricted to religious issues. But in practice, Judaism made no clear distinction between religious and secular spheres. American Jews transformed old institutions into forms appropriate to their new setting. Gradually, community power drifted from the rabbinate, and dispute settlement began to function as an instrument of immigration acculturation rather than as a shield to protect religious isolation. Israel Goldstein, a prominent New York conservative rabbi, was one of several individuals who began an arbitration court in the Jewish community in New York City. He defended his Jewish Conciliation Court for its vital role in the Americanization process of many Jewish immigrant families. As Jews capitalized upon their unprecedented opportunities in the United States, they developed a boundless love affair with American law. Traditionally, religious law had preserved the Jewish community; in the United States, secular law provided an escape from it. There are communities today in which Jews are restrained from engaging in litigation with each other, including Hasidic Williamsburg (Brooklyn) and the Diamond Dealers Club (Manhattan)—a venerated enclave that combines commercialism with Talmudic ethics.

The replacement of communal values by the desire for personal gain is well documented in the history of the United States. Once commercial interactions between strangers supplanted value-based interactions between people who knew each other by their first names, the formal legal system became dominant, and it continues in that position today.

The formal legal system embraces rhetoric between competing attorneys as the pathway to truth. However, this is not the only way to determine truth. I cite two examples:

First, in Bhatgaon, a Fijian Indian community, *pancayat* sessions (literally "council of five") are held to resolve disputes.[8] Pancayats involve direct talk about specific events and personalities. Allegations that, in most contexts, would lead to revenge are discussed at length and without repercussions. While factual evidence is presented, the presentation is managed in such a way that neither party will be completely vanquished. In marked contrast to American courtrooms, there is no adversarial questioning. Testimony establishes a single and noncontradictory account of crucial events. These publicly accomplished facts are seen to stand on their own merit. The disputants usually shake hands, which serves as both a public statement of the resumption of amicable relationships between them and a signal that the session is over. A cooperative and binding account of a contested

8. Brenneis, "Dramatic Gestures."

incident is accomplished, and interested villagers are left to draw their own conclusions and interpretations. A broader discussion of pancayats is included in a later chapter.

The second example is the justice system in France,[9] which employs an *inquisitorial* protocol, under which an investigating judge has the central fact-finding responsibilities before trial. The trial judges employ the file built during the investigation—including statements of witnesses and the defendants themselves—in directing the proceedings. When cases are brought to trial, the presiding judges (as well as both prosecuting and defense counsel) have before them the complete dossiers—all the results of prior investigative efforts. The French *inquisitorial* system stands in stark contract to the *accusatorial* procedures of the formal legal system in the United States.

The Circle process is a way in which dialogue can replace argumentation when dealing with individuals who have broken laws or community expectations. Healing can replace punishment, the word "neighbor" can again be considered to have real value, first names can replace group labels, and the communal good can again be elevated to a position of respect.

The Dominant Thinking Process in Our Culture

Now, let's consider how the dominant thinking process in our culture arose, and how it colors the way in which we interact with each other.

The Dialectic and the Debate Process

Aristotle developed and practiced the art of the dialectic, or logical argument, as a method for determining which premises a person would be likely to concede. The teachings of Christ, as articulated in church doctrine, had to be protected against heresies, so the clergy was trained in the skills of disputation—the dialectic. Most famous universities in Europe were originally church institutions, so the dialectic culture was handed down, and impacts our style of thinking today.

While the purpose of the dialectic has historically been to discern the truth, the procedure is sometimes confused with debate that, in the formal

9. Frankel, *Partisan Justice*, 42.

legal system, is used to convince those with adjudicatory authority of the strength of an argument.

Edward de Bono sharply condemns the Western argumentative model:

> It is a totally absurd Western thinking idiom that attack is a sufficient generative and design system. . . .
>
> The danger is that we actually believe that argument is a way of creating, designing and building up an idea. This is quite simply nonsense. If the argument mode is the only mode available in normal conflict situations then it is no wonder that there is so little creative design.[10]

Although debate is easy to enact, comfortable to use, and makes winners feel good, it puts all non-winners and their ideas on the waste pile, and precludes discovery of those nuggets of wisdom on which momentous cultural breakthroughs are based. Rather than focusing on winners and losers, doesn't it make sense to focus instead on what is of value in *all* ideas, and on how to work collaboratively to make those ideas better? The Circle process provides time and space for this to happen.

Critical versus Creative Thinking

We have traditionally placed more value on teaching critical thinking skills than on teaching creative thinking skills. We can measure intelligence and can see its manifestations in school tests, so we focus on them. We cannot easily measure creative thinking skills, including such things as exploration and wisdom, and so we tend to ignore them. If someone's idea is 90 percent worthwhile and 10 percent of questionable value, the tendency in our culture is to focus critically on the 10 percent and nitpick it—usually because the idea is not our own. If we deign to acknowledge the idea at all, we seek to improve it by tweaking its shortcomings with cleverness, rather than by giving credit to the owner and then openly and creatively building on its positive points. Constantly improving horse-drawn carriages did not lead to the invention of the automobile.

The Circle process provides time and space for the emergence of creative ideas, and for building on and improving those ideas. The Circle

10. De Bono, *Conflicts*, 21–23.

process provides a forum in which there are no winners or losers—only the opportunity for developing and expanding on ideas.

Our Linear Culture and Its Shortfalls

We live in a linear, solution-focused culture, and it is this pattern that has allowed the United States to excel in science, technology, and business development. We identify a need, analyze it, establish goals, and implement a solution. With the advances of the Industrial Revolution, the Scientific Revolution, and now the Electronic Communication Revolution, the United States is considered by many people to be a leader in innovation—and the characterization is justified. Monetary gain in the United States is typically tied to technological achievements, and such gain is usually attained by the linear progression from design to production to marketing to sales.

Yet, in spite of these amazing technological and commercial achievements, we live in a society in which people are pummeled with thirty-second sound bites with no opportunity for dialogue (meaningful conversation between two or more people); in which people discount the value of listening to others; a society of increased contentiousness between neighbors; leaders beholden to special interest groups in exchange for personal gain; politicians mired in stagnant paradigms; increased incarceration of citizens; and armed conflicts around the world. We live in a time of a burgeoning need for food pantries, and of increasing numbers of mental health patients. Joseph Stiglitz points up the fact that we are experiencing a widening schism between those with abundant wealth and those who are "getting by" or living on public assistance.[11] Add to the above list from your own personal experience bank. Clearly, our linear culture is not serving us well.

Communication technology now allows all interactions to be by texting on electronic devices. This format precludes the opportunity to explore new ideas in depth, removes or perhaps prevents the involvement of emotions in human interactions, and eliminates the opportunity to clarify intentions. Only with face-to-face contact is it possible to hear, see, feel, and learn from the stories expressed by voice intonations, facial expressions, and kinesics (body language). Yes, technologies such as Skype are emerging, but a video image is a poor substitute for human contact.

---

11. Stiglitz, *Price of Inequality.*

Ross emphasizes that, in an age when technology can both instantly create and instantly discard items and trends, care must be taken to consider people as resources that must be protected and nurtured:

> We, on our linear path, live under the illusion that we can simply throw away the byproducts of production, distribution and consumption that disturb us. We seem to take the same attitude towards those people who disturb us. We pretend that we can put them out of sight too, that they will never come back to haunt or disturb us, and that we can ignore whatever factors produced their dysfunction. Just as Native people traditionally viewed their relationship with the environment as a circular one requiring much attention to maintaining a healthy balance, so too, I suggest, do they approach people as "resources" which all will need, and as entities which are worthwhile in themselves and for that reason alone deserve to be nurtured.[12]

Meaningful interactions between human beings are not linear. Their color arises from proposing ideas, listening to responses, parrying, creating, building, and learning. We thirst for a forum in which people can articulate their needs, desires, and dreams; can shout for joy when they want; can openly express grief; can float off-the-wall new ideas without fear of castigation; and can have assurance of being listened to. Linear processes can achieve technological advances, but they cannot resolve relationship issues. The Circle process provides such a forum.

Summary

Debate is a waste of time, energy, and creative potential, and should be relegated to the shelves of history, if indeed the good of communities is our goal. It is the prospering of individuals within communities, and of communities themselves, on which we should be focusing our energy and aspirations.

Creative thinking is the fertile field in which new solutions to problems can be cultivated. Creative thinking should be taught to students of all ages and fostered in all facets of our personal, social, and professional lives.

Human relationships are not linear. Relationships change with each interaction, and such interactions cannot be programmed on a computer. Electronic communication devices now allow operators to sit in physical

12. Ross, *Dancing with a Ghost*, 162–63.

isolation and consider that words on a screen equate to meaningful dialogue. Electronic communication can be valuable for conducting business, and may enhance relationships in some situations, but it precludes the benefits of seeing the rich nuances of face-to-face sharing of words—with their pauses and intonations, and emotions shown kinesically.

We hunger for a forum in which dialogue replaces debate, creativity trumps criticism, and the agenda is not the prime driver—nor time the limiting factor. The Circle process offers the opportunity for the bonding of people and groups, and for building of bridges between groups of people. The Circle process offers a key to unlocking the kernels of wisdom inherent in all individuals, and it is with those kernels that a positive community future can be built. Only by being face-to-face with people, and by listening intently to their stories, can we understand their needs, desires, and dreams. Without face-to-face interactions, individuals and groups have no choice but to revert to reliance on their rights—as codified in the formal legal system (and international law). Placing people's rights ahead of their needs, desires, and dreams is neither correct nor wise. The Circle process offers a way for people to express their humanness, and provides a positive and powerful alternative to the status quo.

5

Where Would We Like to Go?

I ENVISION FOUR OPTIONS, but you are invited to expand this list. First, we could revert to the mores of small communities embraced during the seventeenth century in the northeastern United States. Second we could carry on with the current contentious manner in which issues are discussed and the top-down way in which many decisions are made. Third, we could support ways of resolving conflicts that are alternatives to the formal legal system. Finally, we could build on all of the ideas that have worked in the past, and creatively design a new and better way for interacting with each other and for resolving difficulties between individuals and groups. Let's look at each of these options.

Small Community Mores

This option would require living in small population units without modern electronic communication devices. Citizens would agree on norms of community behavior, and deviations from those norms would be handled within the communities. This is the pattern instituted by the Massachusetts Bay Colony and other colonies in New England prior to the advent of mercantilism.[1] Although some current-day communal living arrangements achieve a degree of success in so doing, these groups are commonly bound by faith principles that do not translate to a large percentage of the population of the United States.

---

1. Auerbach, *Justice without Law.*

Accepting the Status Quo

This option would accept vigilantism by individuals and groups as a means of resolving differences, with policing agencies governing actions and the formal legal system arbitrating disagreements. It is commonly agreed that the formal legal system is a robust adjudicator for all situations in which the "law" has been broken, and hence it is an accepted controller of vigilantism. Internationally, organizations such as the United Nations and the International Criminal Court have been authorized to adjudicate issues of human rights within countries, and some disagreements between countries. Vigilantism, in its many colors, can be restrained by codifying rights and upholding them, and in some cases by the pressure of public opinion and/ or the use of force. The above processes are valid applications of formal legal systems, but the emphasis placed on constraints and on punishment for past actions precludes recognition of the potential of human beings for developing new and even better ways for resolving differences.

Alternatives to the Formal Legal System

Mediation is a widely recognized alternative to the formal legal system, and is one form of "alternative dispute resolution" (ADR). As a practitioner, I speak heartily in favor of mediation as an effective way in which to guide parties toward the goal(s) they have set—if they so choose, without doing battle in the courts. I here propose the term "cooperative conflict resolution" (CCR) for mediation, in place of ADR, as a more meaningful descriptor of mediation as a positive, stand-alone process that is not an alternative to anything—including the formal legal system.

Other suggested alternatives to the formal legal system include: settlement conferences (in which a settlement master, usually a lawyer, hears the arguments of both parties and advises how the decision would probably play out if the dispute were to go to court); arbitration (a non-court-related, binding or non-binding adjudicatory process); court-annexed arbitration; private tribunals (rent-a-judge process); med-rec (a process that begins as mediation but in which, if the parties do not reach an agreement, a recommendation is made to the court); mini trials (abbreviated presentation of evidence to one or more expert neutral facilitators or other parties with decision-making authority); and summary jury trials (abbreviated presentation of complex issues to one or more advisory juries, who then render one or more advisory verdicts for parties with decision-making authority to consider in their settlement discussions).

These alternatives alleviate court dockets, but the question is validly raised whether participants in such alternative processes receive a lesser quality of justice than that provided by the formal legal system. The same question applies to quasi-legal programs such as neighborhood conciliation boards, neighborhood tribunals, and self-help legal offices staffed by academic students of the law—all alternatives guaranteed to reserve the formal legal system for those citizens not disadvantaged by race, class, age, national origin, or economic ability. Is a two-tiered justice approach truly a valid alternative to the formal legal system?

A Better Approach

Building on Good Ideas

A fourth option is to build on the good points of all existing processes, including the wisdom of indigenous cultures, which is available to us without charge and can be put forward as a positive framework for collaboratively resolving conflicts. In the Sandy Lake Reserve in northwestern Ontario, for example, an experiment was conducted in 1991 to marry the traditional native justice system and the existing outside system.[2] A judge, clerk, and recorder sat on one side of a square set of tables; an elder and interpreter sat to the right; defense lawyers, offenders, and their families, together with probation officers, sat across from the judge; and the Crown attorney and police officers sat to the left of the judge.

> The Elders bring to the court their knowledge of the accused and his or her family circumstances, and their appreciation of the specific events which might have contributed to the commission of the offense. . . . the Elders seldom speak about the transgression itself, about the past. They focus instead upon the future, upon restoration of peaceful relations. They do not speak of punishment, but they do focus upon compensation and restitution to the victim, upon "making things right again." . . . They do not make threatening noises about what might happen to offenders if they repeat their misbehavior. Instead, they remind them of how important they are to their family and their community, and about the contributions they can make in the future. They also talk about

2. Ross, *Dancing with a Ghost.*

the help that they and others stand ready to provide to assist each person to realize his or her potential. At every step it seems as though the underlying message is that each person before the court can, with guidance, counseling and sustained effort on their own part, come closer to realizing the *goodness* that lies within them. . . . At every step they tell each offender they meet with not about how hard he'll have to work to control his base self but instead how they are there to help him realize the goodness that is within him.[3]

It is not necessary to tear down *any* existing structure. As Edward de Bono points out, it is a waste of human time, energy, and talent to do so.[4] Instead, let's take the best of everything that is in our collective experience bank and use it to design and build a better future. In the space below, rather than cherry-picking the positive aspects of existing structures and building on them, I am going to expand the discussion by considering three well-grounded fields of inquiry—mathematics, communication science, and the creative process—and, with examples, show how collaboration and expansive thinking can lead to the development of exciting new possibilities.

Three creative ideas that have been developed relatively recently, and that focus on human interactions, are: (1) the "Adjusted Winner" procedure;[5] (2) the reflective dialogue process developed by the Public Conversations Project;[6] and (3) the Supranational Independent Thinking Organization (SITO), an international conflict management model proposed by Edward de Bono.[7]

The design of the above three processes was made possible by providing time and space for people to speak without being criticized, and to listen intently, respond respectfully, and build creatively on the ideas raised by others. The Circle process provides the time and space in which such creative contributions can be made. Let's look more closely at the Adjusted Winner procedure, the Public Conversations Project, and the SITO model to better understand the power that collaboration can achieve.

3. Ibid., 167–69.
4. De Bono, *Conflicts*.
5. Brams and Taylor, *Fair Division*.
6. Stains, "Reflection for Connection."
7. De Bono, *Conflicts*.

The Adjusted Winner Procedure

Stephen Brams and Alan Taylor developed a mathematical procedure for dividing things fairly, which can be used to divide such items as marital property, and to decide on issues such as child custody, visitation rights, and spousal support.[8] I cite an example of the Adjusted Winner procedure's power for dividing things fairly and for achieving the equitable, envy-free, and efficient division of marital property.[9] Each party is given one hundred points to distribute between three items (an antique chest, a car, and a watercolor painting), according to their own values—such as sentimentality, family history, financial need, and aspirations. The division is equitable because the parties receive the same number of points, envy free because neither party would trade his or her allocation for that of the other, and efficient because both parties receive greater value than if they had simply divided the points equally. The couples in my mediation experience realize that they have received the items of greatest value to them, and appreciate having been given the opportunity to participate in what they consider to be a fair process.

I have also applied the Adjusted Winner procedure to (1) a hypothetical public policy dispute between a contractor with plans to build a new community (consisting of houses, business structures, and an athletic field), and the residents of an adjacent existing neighborhood; (2) an environmental dispute involving a proposed mine, with concerns over groundwater quality, airborne emissions, noise, traffic, reclamation, and economic impacts; and (3) the division of a 100,000 square mile country during a lull in a war between three ethnic groups.[10] In the third example, before the war, one of the factions raised sheep, the second lived in the mountains and mined iron ore, and the third lived in the major city and made the iron ore into steel. Representatives of the three factions met with a neutral party in a neutral venue and jointly divided the map of the country into one hundred square mile parcels. Each faction then allocated one thousand points to the parcels—according to their culture, their historical means of sustenance, and any other factors of importance to them. The sheepherders allocated a small number of points to each of a large number of land parcels suitable for grazing, the mining faction allocated all of its points to just ten

8. Brams and Taylor, *Fair Division*.

9. Lavery, "Mathematics and Mediation?," 4–5.

10. Lavery, "Dividing Things Fairly," 4–5.

parcels of land in the mountains, and the industrial faction allocated all of its points to only five parcels in and surrounding the city. The parties then revealed their point allocations as a starting point for discussions of how to best achieve everyone's highest-priority goals. The Adjusted Winner procedure may or may not resolve *all* of the land division issues, but it *will* resolve many of them. Moreover, the positive experience of working together may well lead to a constructive dialogue on how to resolve the rest. Considering the cost in human lives caused by war, perhaps it's time to try another approach. The Adjusted Winner procedure is an approach worthy of consideration and, yes, the Circle process can ease the discussion of the contentious issues.

The Public Conversations Project

Laura Chasin and four associates initiated the Public Conversations Project (PCP) in 1989.[11] Since then, PCP has pioneered a distinctive and effective approach that shifts communication from being a debate to a dialogue, with its goals being enhanced understanding, repaired relationships, and rebuilt trust.[12, 13] Drawing on mediation fundamentals, traditional conflict resolution methods, and consensus building, PCP has developed reflective dialogue practices that have been tested throughout the world in a broad field of conflicts, including the abortion controversy, the future of the northern forests in New England, women's health issues, and church membership based on sexual preference.

The principles of PCP are the same ones in the Circle process embraced by Community Circles, although PCP does not use a talking piece to regulate conversation, and uses a scripted format for discussion so that resolution of issues can be achieved within a defined time frame. Guidelines are agreed on by the group, questions are posed that ask participants to look deeply at their feelings and their often entrenched opinions, responses are voiced, ideas are floated, discussions are held, and decisions are made—if decisions are the goal of the group. Pauses for self-reflection before, during, and after dialogue are a key component of the process and are built in at specific times by the group facilitators. The precepts of PCP are: (1) *Stop*. Slow down. Take a rest from the breakneck pace of feeling, thinking,

11. Public Conversations Project training manual.
12. Ibid.
13. Stains, "Reflection for Connection."

and speaking. (2) *Look*. Notice that which has fallen into the shadows or been rendered invisible by the editing power of an oft-told story about who "they" are, who you are, and the history of the relationship. (3) *Listen*. Listen for what you care about—what your purposes are, in the immediate situation and at a higher level in your life. (4) *Decide*. Develop intentions for the ways you want to speak and listen in your next encounter—ways that will best help you understand others and be understood, and that best embody your commitments and hopes. The focus of PCP, as in all Circle processes, is on the enhancement of relationships. Improved relationships make problem solving a much easier task.

During the PCP training I attended, a contentious issue posed to the group was the divide between members of a church over whether or not to become a "truly welcoming church," in which gays and lesbians would not only be tolerated but embraced as full members, where their sexual orientation would be accepted, and their committed partner relationships would be honored.

The first question posed by the training facilitator to each of the small Circles of trainees was designed to connect participants' initial feelings about the situation with their own personal experience: "Can you tell us something about your life experiences or current situation that will help us understand your views and concerns about the welcoming church issue?" The next questions encouraged participants to reflect on aspects of their own views that they may not express as readily as their usual views, and that reveal fresh information about complex thinking that may provide insights for connections across different views and new perspectives: "Do you have any uncertainties or mixed feelings about any of the views you have held in the past? Are their any gray areas in how you feel? Can you say something about both the certainties and uncertainties you bring to this conversation?" Other questions posed by the facilitator included: "Have you ever felt stereotyped by those who hold different views on this issue? If so, how? Which of these stereotypes was most painful to you, most accurate? Why? And have you ever had a constructive conversation about sexual preferences with someone who has very different views? If you have, what made that conversation possible?" Reflective time was provided before participants responded to each question.

During the above process, people were guided to interact as individuals instead of as members of a labeled group—e.g., "straight" or "gay". Questions were designed to help people move from a restrictive "old conversation" to an expansive "new conversation" that allowed them to see issues in a new light, based on the views and feelings expressed by others. Because the conversations were confidential, people felt comfortable sharing not only their strong feelings, but also their uncertainties about their stated positions.

A meaningful dialogue offers participants the opportunity to speak and be listened to in a respectful manner, to develop mutual understanding, to learn about the perspectives of others, and to reflect on one's own views. The Circle format used in the training exercise was a powerful way in which to accomplish the goal of the training program.

SITO (Supranational Independent Thinking Organization)

John Horgan's detailed research on the causes of war concluded that there is no clear-cut genetic or cultural predisposition for aggression.[14] Further, there is no clear-cut data that support most aggression being caused by dense populations and scarce resources (Malthus), or by the struggle between "haves" and "have-nots" (Marx).

> Warfare is "an invention," she concludes, like cooking, writing, or marriage. Once a society becomes exposed to the "idea" of war, then "they will sometimes go to war" under certain circumstances.[15]

> Over and over, warmongering leaders have exploited the docility, bounded rationality, and altruism of their subjects and manipulated them into hating and attacking outsiders, and even each other.[16]

Regardless of the reason or reasons for wars, disagreements between people and nations do exist and will continue to arise, and finding a good way to defuse them should be a preeminent pursuit of mankind. Edward de Bono proposes a new organization, SITO, as a good way to defuse international conflicts.[17] He further submits the proposition that the United Nations, the Red Cross, private groups such as the Quakers, democratic governments, bureaucracies, and the Vatican are inadequate structures for the job.

14. Horgan, *End of War.*
15. Ibid., 102.
16. Ibid., 122.
17. De Bono, *Conflicts,* 183–96.

Considered more closely, the United Nations uses a jury system for deciding on actions. The jury system can work only if the peers are uninvolved in the case. As soon as nations form into real or de facto alliances, the jury system becomes unworkable. In short, the United Nations has become a sort of parliament—what our party advocates is right and what the other party advocates is wrong. Matters can no longer be decided on their merits because party loyalty comes first. Instead of constructive design, there is attack and defense and the parading of righteousness.

The Red Cross does not suffer the disadvantages of being a representational body, as with the United Nations. Its focus on humanitarian work, however, precludes its use as an effective design structure for developing new possibilities for defusing aggression.

The Quakers have done admirable work mediating between warring factions. Their expertise in lubricating conversations between adversaries is valuable, but does not rise to the status of third-party involvement in a creative thinking exercise—what de Bono terms "triangular thinking."[18]

In democracies, once a conflict has been declared with another entity, there is a tendency to close ranks in a partisan manner. To not support the troops is sabotage and shameful. The thinking mode of democracies is argumentation, and the probability of moving to a creative mode is remote.

Bureaucrats achieve success by following established rules and by not making mistakes. With the task being to look for an organization that could play an effective role in the resolution of conflicts, consideration must be given to the fact that well-developed administrative skills within bureaucracies are of no value to the process of designing new conflict resolution tools.

The Vatican has historically played a role in some disputes between countries. But the enlargement of the cultural world map to now include China, African nations, and a number of other developing countries makes the dominant Western focus of the Vatican of lesser importance in resolving conflicts than it once was.

Having now disparaged some of the major international organizations in the search for good ways in which to defuse, manage, and resolve conflicts, it's time to bring to center stage de Bono's proposed Supranational Independent Thinking Organization (SITO), in which the emphasis is on creative design. The SITO model functions outside of politics, ideologies, and nations. It is not a representational body, and there are no member

18. Ibid., 124.

nations as voting delegates. SITO is free from allegiances or dependencies. It focuses directly on the art and activity of thinking—about conflict and other issues of global concern. SITO offers a designed-outcome approach that replaces the argumentation mode for discussing and resolving conflicts. The individuals who participate in SITO are carefully chosen, act as individuals and not as members of any group, and are uniquely trained to provide creative ideas on how to resolve conflicts. Just one of the positive attributes of the SITO model is that it is ideally positioned to provide an outside view of conflict situations. While combatants are deeply mired and unable to see a way out, SITO is able to see both the details and the larger context within which the conflict is occurring. SITO representatives can perform the role of a neutral third party who, rather than being a passive mediator, is an active guide in proposing possible alternatives, suggesting directions for solutions, and guiding the parties to an acceptable designed outcome that makes sense to all parties. An example posed by de Bono is the approach of calculating the cost of a *planned* intervention—in terms of lives lost, dollars (or other currency) to be expended, reconstruction costs to be incurred, social impacts to be endured, and the negative ramifications of reputation scarring. The group considering intervention could then use this information in its decision-making process to determine whether intervention should or should not take place. SITO could set up task forces and organize conferences, conduct research, and be an umbrella organization to coordinate individual diplomatic efforts.

Although de Bono proposed the SITO model in 1985, support by the international community has not materialized. The idea is worthy of renewed attention, however, in an era in which war is causing tremendous and senseless loss of life, and exorbitant expenditure of monetary resources.

Summary

We must agree to end our absorption with punishment for past actions, and to redirect our energy toward designing better ways of communicating with each other and better ways of managing and resolving conflicts. We must ramp up our compassion for those who have been harmed, and develop restorative methods of accountability for those who have caused harm. We must reintegrate wrongdoers into our communities instead of isolating them and losing their potential valuable contributions. We must learn to listen more acutely and to tolerate thoughts, ideas, and even religious beliefs different from our own. And finally, we must acknowledge that it is our responsibility as citizens, and not the responsibility of formal legal systems and governing bodies, to move us toward more peaceful, just, and productive communities. We have the opportunity to change the focus from solving problems by legal means to designing communities in which we choose to live because they provide the necessities of safety, respect, and caring, and because they provide a sense of belonging—in which we can achieve our full potential as human beings.

The Circle process has worked well for thousands of years to achieve the above goals, and can be equally valuable today in the challenging environment of the twenty-first century. The Circle process brings the concepts of possibility and hope into discussions, and removes judgment and debate as wasteful processes that sap the energy and resources of individuals who want desperately to belong to safe and vibrant communities.

6

The Circular Nature of Things

As a proem to our exploration of the Circle process, it's of value to consider Circles themselves. Let's begin our journey with a pad and a pencil. Take a few minutes to list all of the Circles you have encountered in your lifetime, including those you see, feel, taste, use, participate in, and experience on a daily basis. You might start small, with the cross section of a blood vessel and the shape of the iris in your eye; or large, with the sun, visible bodies in the night sky, and satellite views of the earth. Take a break now and begin your list.

Hoses and pipes have circular cross sections. Why? Baseballs and tennis balls are round, wheels are round, Hula Hoops are round, igloos are round, and ball bearings are round. Why? What characteristics of circular things make them important in nature, in technology, and in our daily lives? Does the importance of Circles go beyond the technological structures that make our twenty-first-century lives possible? Do they possibly influence our relationship with the natural world—our spirituality? Do Circles affect how we interact as groups of individuals? Do they impact how we interact as nations? Why do we gather in Circles around campfires, while sewing, sharing joy and grief, talking, and telling family stories? How is your list coming along?

Some of the Circles on my list occur in nature: Saturn's rings, tree rings, flowers, ripples on a pond, the moon, lines of latitude, maple seeds spiraling to the ground, and fairy Circles. The four seasons and the stages of life are circular. Other Circles occur in art: spirals, mandalas, the color wheel, drums, Leonardo de Vinci's *Vitruvian Man* drawing, wedding bands, Olympic Circles, and pottery. Venerable buildings such as the Pantheon in Rome, the Sultan Ahmed Mosque in Istanbul, the Guggenheim Museum in New York, and the Nott Memorial Library on the campus of Union College in Schenectady, New York, are circular, as is the dome of the National Museum of the American Indian. Circles in science and technology include: clock gears, steering wheels, water wheels, millstones, manhole covers, traffic Circles, nanotubes, optical lenses, compasses, bicycle wheels, carousels, and supercolliders. Circles we find in past and present cultures include: stone and timber Circles, the Buddhist Wheel of Life, the Bighorn Medicine Wheel in Wyoming, and tepee rings. Circles also occur in the animate nonhuman world, as reported by Carl Zimmer.

> A group of dolphin moms will often form circles around their calves, perhaps protecting them from predators. "We call them playpens," Wells says.[1]

Is it just by chance that Circles occur so commonly in the natural world? Does it not behoove us to consider more carefully the potential value and power that Circles can bring to our interactions with other human beings?

It has been claimed by mathematicians that Circles are symbols that exist only as mental constructs, and that they are not things in themselves. Points of agreement between mathematicians and laypersons, however, are that Circles precede written history, are the basis for many of the good things that humankind has created, and pervade and enrich all aspects of our lives.

1. Zimmer, "Friends with Benefits," 3.

7
A Circles Prologue

WE'LL BEGIN WITH AN overview of the Circle process and its indigenous roots. We'll then discuss the Circle foundation of our political system in the United States, and will list some of the types of Circles that can be convened. The ways in which the Circle process can be used in human interactions will be addressed in the chapter on applications of the Circle process.

Overview

The Stonehenge archeological site in England is well known, and many people attest to its spiritual significance. Recent excavations in southeastern Turkey, at a place called Gobekli Tepe, have unearthed at least sixteen megaliths—circular arrangements of carved stones—that are almost eleven thousand years old and predate Stonehenge by some six thousand years. To put the date of Gobekli Tepe in perspective, the massive stones—comprising possibly the world's oldest temple—were crafted before the development of metal tools or even pottery.[1]

Our current consideration of Circles and their significance is but a tiny dot on the time line of history. The Circle process has been used for thousands of years to understand the natural world; to build, reinforce, and heal relationships; to share wisdom by telling and listening to stories; to develop an understanding of needs, desires, and dreams; to craft solutions to problems; and to work toward possibilities. The Circle process is based on the connectedness of all things. A vital part of the Circle process is the encouragement of healthy connections among Circle participants and within communities. The well-being of each individual is directly connected to the well-being of others and the well-being of the community.

1. Curry, "Gobekli Tepe."

Circles are non-judgmental places—places for caring, for honoring the dignity of all beings, and for supporting and receiving support. Circles are inclusive. There is shared leadership in many cultures, with no distinction between leader and follower, or teacher and student. There are direct sight and sound lines between participants, making it easy to listen to the words spoken and the feelings expressed. The structure of the Circle focuses attention on the participants and the tasks for which the Circle has been convened. The Circle links all participants, and encourages a sense of shared effort and common purpose. A talking piece is employed in many cultures to regulate conversation, with the intent being to eliminate domination of discussions by a small number of people. The Circle process lets the group know that the meeting is committed to hearing everyone's views. When a problem or an issue is brought to the Circle, it is placed in the center and is owned by everyone. It is not simply a unique or different set of procedures that make Circles work; it is the collective will of all participants to share the difficulties of moving through issues to seek understanding, to heal, and to create a caring, respectful community. Circles foster a sacred quality to the words spoken and the feelings expressed. The term "sacred" as used here means revered, respected, protected, and secure.

Each person has a wealth of knowledge and experience, and we cannot afford to dismiss anyone's contribution. Each person's input could hold the key to a solution that no one else saw. The Circle process allows the contributions of everyone to be listened to and considered. With this format, it is much less likely that those people with opposing views will dig in just to make a point. Power plays do not occur. Circle members feel safe and respected, which allows them to take risks in reaching out to each other. They can yield when necessary, and also dare to be creative. Masks worn in public can be discarded without fear of embarrassment or retribution.

Some of the benefits of the Circle process are:

- Encouraging all interests to be represented and respected

- Building understanding and respect for differing opinions

- Allowing parties to deal directly with each other

- Providing an equal voice for all parties

- Practicing positive communication patterns

- Moving from the "old conversation" to a "new and more fruitful conversation"

- Providing a safe environment that generates frank, honest, and re-spectful exchanges of fears, concerns, interests, needs, desires, and aspirations
- Providing a forum that builds improved working relationships, forges new partnerships, and fosters cooperative, innovative problem-solving
- Incorporating a broad span of interests that reflects the collective ef-forts of all participants
- Rejecting judgment, and building only on the positive ideas of members
- Reaching collective-intelligence group decisions
- Garnering the commitment of all participants to successfully imple-ment group decisions
- Participating in a true democracy

Circles support the core values of humanity. They give people the op-portunity to be listened to and, by that gesture, unlock their strength to be able to resolve their own issues and develop compassion for others.

Our Indigenous Roots

It is fitting to build this section on quotations from three indigenous writ-ers, and to conclude it with the words of Rupert Ross—an individual who guided fishing charters in northern Ontario for eleven years, and then em-barked on a successful career as a Crown attorney working with indigenous communities.

> Then I was standing on the highest mountain of them all, and round about beneath me was the whole hoop of the world. And while I stood there I saw more than I can tell and I understood more than I saw; for I was seeing in a sacred manner the shapes of all things in the spirit, and the shape of all shapes as they must live together like one being. And I saw that the sacred hoop of my people was one of many hoops that made one circle, wide as day-light and as starlight, and in the center grew one mighty flowering tree to shelter all the children of one mother and one father. And I saw that it was holy.[2]

2. Neihardt, *Black Elk Speaks*, 33.

You have noticed that everything an Indian does is in a circle, and that is because the Power of the World always works in circles, and everything tries to be round. . . . Everything the Power of the World does is done in a circle. The sky is round, and I have heard that the earth is round like a ball, and so are all the stars. The Wind, in its greatest power, whirls. Birds make their nests in circles, for theirs is the same religion as ours. The sun comes forth and goes down again in a circle. The Moon does the same, and both are round. Even the seasons form a great circle in their changing, and always come back again to where they were. The life of a man is a circle from childhood to childhood and so it is in everything where power moves.[3]

For most indigenous cultures throughout the world, circles play a significant role both in the symbolic realm (including their use in teaching and ceremonies) and the practical domain (through their use in problem solving and as a structure for discussions). In our cultural teachings as Native people, we understand that circles are a part of the natural order of creation and thus should be an important part of our lives. The circle, often referred to as the Medicine Wheel or sacred hoop, is one of our primary teaching symbols. We are often told that in one lifetime we cannot collect all the teachings that this symbol holds for us. One of the fundamental teachings of the Medicine Wheel is that it is divided into four quadrants, making up our being as humans.[4]

There are many different ways that this basic concept is expressed: the four grandfathers, the four winds, the four cardinal directions, and many other relationships that can be expressed in sets of four. . . . The Medicine Wheel teaches us that the four symbolic races are all part of the same human family. All are brothers and sisters living on the same Mother Earth. The Medicine Wheel teaches us that the four elements, each so distinctive and powerful, are all part of the physical world. All must be respected equally for their gift of life. The Medicine Wheel teaches us that we have four aspects to our nature: the physical, the mental, the emotional, and the spiritual. Each of these aspects must be equally developed in a healthy, well-balanced individual through the development and use of volition (i.e. will).[5]

3. Ibid., 155–56.
4. Eagle, "Journey in Aboriginal Restorative Justice," 6–7.
5. Bopp, *Sacred Tree*, 9–12.

More and more people are recognizing the value of using the Circle process in dealing with conflict on many levels. My personal point of view is that it restores pride in individuals and our nation when we can claim that this process has been ours all along, that it was taken from us and that now we have the opportunity to restore it.[6]

Rupert Ross offers the following insights from his research on aboriginal justice:

> What was it that those Ojibway elders *did* want to tell their researchers about? . . . "Respect for each other and a universal appreciation for the power of the creator kept everyone walking down a path that encompassed honesty, truths, respect for everything in their immediate life or ecosystem, whether it was your fellow man or beast or plant life. It was a holistic respect for everything that the Anishinaabeg could see, smell, hear, taste and feel."
>
> If we move to the other side of the continent, to the Salish people of western Washington, we come across similar types of messages. . . . "Children learned from birth the proper attitudes and behaviors that promoted appropriate dispute *prevention and resolution*: to respect their elders and teachers, to refrain from boastfulness, and to value qualities of self-discipline, self-control, generosity, peacefulness and hospitality. . . . Their teachers were usually the family elders who taught by example, lecture, storytelling, and recounting family history. This training prepared children for their role in a society that was structured to *minimize* open disputing."
>
> So, there it was: within traditional Aboriginal understandings, a justice system involved far more than simply controlling how disputes were handled after they broke out. *Instead, the primary emphasis was on teaching individuals from birth how to live together in ways that avoided or minimized them in the first place.* . . . justice involves far more than what you do after things have gone wrong. Instead, it involves creating the social conditions that minimize such wrongdoing. . . .
>
> I also remember something a Cree man said at a justice conference in Alberta in 1991. . . . "Why does your law, from the Ten Commandments to the Criminal Code, speak only about what people should not *do*? Why don't your laws speak to people about what they should *be*?"[7]

6. Eagle, "Journey in Aboriginal Restorative Justice," 8.
7. Ross, *Returning to the Teachings*, 254–57.

The Circle Foundation of Our Political System

The political foundation of the United States was shaped primarily by two strong Circle traditions: the British and the Native American. One of Britain's most enduring stories, originating in Celtic mythology, is that of King Arthur and his Round Table. The knights took an oath to serve not only the other Round Table members but also the kingdom as a whole. Their covenant promised a humane safety net for even the most vulnerable members of society.

When we consider the history of the US Constitution, we learn that it was based fundamentally on the model of the Iroquois Confederacy—a kinship state consisting of separate tribal representatives who met in a council Circle every five years, with the responsibility for the welfare of the whole. Female tribal leaders formulated the issues and questions to be debated, and appointed male delegates and deputies to speak for clans at tribal councils. The laws of the Confederacy insured the Great Peace and protected the individual rights, safety, and justice of members.

Donald Grunde and Kathryn McConnell relate the importance of spirituality, nature, and relationships in the Iroquois culture; and highlight the role that Benjamin Franklin played in bringing Iroquois values to bear in the drafting of the US Constitution:

> The philosophy of the Iroquois was based on the concept that all life is unified spiritually with the natural environment and other forces surrounding the people. . . . The spiritual power of only one individual was limited, but when combined with the other individuals of the hearth, otiianer, or clan, the spiritual power became strong.[8]

> Washington—Benjamin Franklin, one of the original architects of the United States government, introduced as a model for the country's framework document the constitution of the Iroquois Nation, according to a Smithsonian Institution specialist of American Indian History. The Iroquois, a North American Indian confederacy of several tribes, allied with some of the first European settlers of what later became the United States. The Iroquois' detailed constitution—called the Great Law of Peace—guaranteed freedom of religion and expression and other rights later embraced in the U.S. Constitution, . . . the Iroquois document also presented to framers of the U.S. Constitution the concept of a two-house legislature

8. Grunde, *Iroquois*, 2.

and a combined government structure of state jurisdictions and a national government. According to the Iroquois constitution, states were first to solve disputes between them on their own. If resolution efforts failed then the national government would take authority, . . . The Great Law said the national government should have a commander-in-chief and that person should present a "state of the union" address to the nation, . . . The Iroquois' also said that when a legislator was presenting an issue to the governing chamber, others should be quiet, a practice adopted by Congress that contrasts with protocol in the British parliament, . . . Franklin, then Pennsylvania's official printer, became familiar with the Iroquois political system by printing minutes of their meetings, . . . "He recognized that the Iroquois constitution contained many features absent in other governments at the time," including the concept that "elected officials were never masters but remained servants of their constituencies," . . . However, the Iroquois constitution differed from the later U.S. document in one important way—it specifically mentioned women. . . . Many Indian nations were matriarchal with women nominating legislators.[9]

One might then ask how the vast number of illiterate colonists knew of democracy since they had no exposure to Plato, Aristotle or John Locke. Perhaps these unread people drew their values in considerable part from the Indian people whom they saw functioning around them. Certainly the white colonists readily used the crops, clothing, and language of the American Indian to cope with the environment. One has the right to believe that they observed the freedom and democracy in Indian society as well.[10]

Circle Designs

Since the time when people sat around tribal fires, we have developed many variations of the Circle process: dialogue groups, Bible study groups, group psychotherapy, twelve-step groups, consciousness-raising Circles, and men's and women's groups, to name a few. According to a study funded by the Gallup Foundation, 40 percent of all adult Americans actively belong to small, voluntary groups whose purpose is to explore what has meaning in their lives, and to address social concerns. Circles convened today give

9. McConnell, "Iroquois Constitution."
10. Grunde, *Iroquois*, xiii.

people the opportunity to learn from each other, and to make decisions that reflect the experience not of one person but the wisdom of a community. Such group decision-making is a mainstay today of successful group processes in all contexts. Circles offer the opportunity for participants to hear about other people's needs, to feel what other people are feeling, and to offer support to them.

A permanent fixture on my cell phone is a photograph of four women sitting in a Circle on a beach in Connecticut, with the sun setting over the water. I met them on the Fourth of July one year, and learned that they had gathered each Tuesday evening during the summer months, on the same beach in the same place, for more than fifteen years. The photograph continually reminds me of the value of Circles—for telling and listening to stories, and for sharing the big issues and the minutiae of our lives.

Think about your current interactions with friends and associates, and consider how the Circle process already plays a role in building a sense of community. Then consider how the Circle process *could* play a more meaningful role in ensuring that all participants have the opportunity to speak uninterrupted, without being judged, and with assurance that their voices will be listened to.

Wisdom Circles

"Wisdom Circles"[11] is an appropriate umbrella term for the many types of Circles that can be convened. Wisdom is "the quality of having experience, knowledge, and good judgment; the quality of being wise."[12] My personal definition of wisdom is: the application of knowledge that allows us to live our lives in a good way. And the sharing of that wisdom is the focus of interactions in each Circle convened.

Whether a Circle is convened for the purpose of talking and listening, sharing ideas, celebrating, healing, grieving, sentencing, solving problems, or peacemaking, the focus is on relationships and on the wisdom we can gain through those relationships. We are all connected, even though, in the hectic pace of our everyday lives, we often lose sight of that connectedness. It is human beings who come together in Circles for a common purpose. It is human beings who assemble to give their energies for the common good. And it is human beings who commit to being members of a community for

11. Garfield et al., *Wisdom Circles*.
12. *New Oxford American Dictionary*.

the purposes of addressing issues, resolving problems, and helping one or more members who are in need.

A Circle convened on behalf of a group of business associates will have a different tone from a Circle convened for a group of friends or family members. And Circles that meet only one time will have a different focus from Circles that meet on a periodic basis. Ongoing Circles might have to consider such specific issues as participant commitment, how to maintain vibrancy, and if and when to disband the Circle. A key to all Circles is that they give participants the chance to move comfortably from blame to understanding, from competition to cooperation, and from debate to dialogue, in so doing building or rebuilding their relationships.

Three types of Circles that might not be familiar to some readers are described below.

Fishbowls

The fishbowl format was developed to accommodate a large number of participants all having an interest in a particular issue. Four or five chairs are arranged in an inner Circle—the fishbowl—with the remaining chairs placed in concentric Circles around the fishbowl. A few participants are selected or self-select to initially be in the fishbowl, while the rest of the group sits outside and listens. In an open fishbowl, one chair is left empty. In a closed fishbowl, all chairs are filled. In an open fishbowl, any member of the audience can, at any time, occupy the empty chair, at which time an existing member of the fishbowl must voluntarily leave and free up a chair. In a closed fishbowl, the initial participants relinquish their chairs after a set amount of time, with other participants then moving into the inner Circle. A facilitator monitors time blocks, supervises scribing of notes, and summarizes the discussion at appropriate times.

Samoan Circles

An innovative Circle format was proposed by Lorenz Aggens, which he named the "Samoan Circle."[13] The Samoan Circle is designed to facilitate the discussion of controversial issues when there is a large group of people interested in a topic. It does not resolve conflicts, although some

13. Aggens, "Origins of the Samoan Circle."

participants have experienced the spontaneous resolution of conflicting views and agreement on actions required, as a result of the contestants in a controversy having listened to one another for the first time. The Samoan Circle is a leaderless meeting. Responsibility for discipline is vested in everyone rather than in a meeting leader. Everyone has a stake in maintaining an orderly environment for discussion. Four chairs are arranged around a circular table in the center of the meeting space, with the remaining chairs placed in concentric Circles. A microphone is placed in the middle of the table to capture the comments made, with it being positioned so there is not a need to pass the microphone from person to person. A moderator opens the meeting, and states that the purpose is to learn from one another as much as is possible about the topic that is at issue—including facts, problems, obstacles, needs, values, possible solutions, suggestions for improvement, and new ideas.

People who want to say something must take a seat at the table. A person taking a seat can join in the discussion, try to change its direction, or raise a new topic. If there are no vacant seats at the table and a person wants to get in on the discussion, he stands near the table until someone gives up a seat. The greater the number of people standing near the table, the stronger the signal to those seated to evaluate their own need to continue to participate. If a person wants to talk to one of the people at the table, he stands directly behind that person's chair as a signal to the others at the table that he wants one of their seats. Discussion can be allowed to run its course if there is no time requirement for adjournment. The meeting room will gradually empty until there may be no more people left at the table, except for an intensely interested group. If a time limit exists, the person who started the meeting can move to the table, wait for a seat to be vacated if none is already empty, and withdraw that chair. Continuing to stand near the table, that person can withdraw each chair as it is vacated.

Individuals can speak without a need for oratorical skill or the ability to put all of their thoughts together into the one, short, cogent statement—which is so often required by the dynamics of large group meetings. In the Samoan Circle, no one person needs to ensure equitable participation, judge fairness, or control people's behavior. The need for participants to use negative labels or to be cheerleaders is lessened. The essence of the Samoan Circle can be captured by an electronic recording device and transcription of the words spoken, or by notes scribed on easel pads on the walls of the room.

A Rectangle—Masquerading as a Circle

The following story speaks to the power of the Circle process—even though there is no circular arrangement of chairs, no central focal object such as a candle, and no defined opening of the Circle with silence, a prayer, or a reading.

I was asked to mediate a family meeting, purportedly convened to discuss how best to support an aging man and his mentally declining wife. Eighteen family members, many of whom had traveled long distances, arrived and seated themselves around a quadrangle of standard conference tables. Factions were apparent, with several relatives who were the couple's primary caregivers comprising one faction, relatives who lived in other towns in the state comprising another faction, and relatives who lived in other states comprising yet a third faction. The members of each faction sat clustered with one another. Another division in the group became apparent—based on religious beliefs—with my own spirituality being brought into question at one point. At times, heated exchanges took place across the quadrangle, and I realized that the underlying issue was more the eventual distribution of the aging couple's assets than their well-being during their final chapter. Sensing the potential for a free-for-all, I decided to call "time out"—one of my perks as a mediator—and suggested the use of a talking piece. I reached into my pocket and withdrew a small stone that I always carry—with the word "peace" engraved on it. I suggested that the stone be passed around the rectangle (i.e., Circle), and that only the person with the stone be allowed to speak. I also suggested the following additional rules: (1) the talking piece could be passed without a person having to speak, (2) there would be no character attacks, and (3) the participants would focus on the needs of the elderly couple. The assembled relatives were initially amused, but did agree to the process guidelines, and the Circle began. In short order, people were listening respectfully, raising issues and concerns in calm tones using non-threatening language, and joking with one another as they shared family stories. Following a break for lunch, the Circle reconvened, with people voluntarily changing the seating pattern, and with the talking piece now affectionately being called "the Rock." Whether a new family custom was begun or not, the use of a talking piece provided a bit of magic for the assembled group.

Whether or not a talking piece is used; and whether a table is rectangular or circular, or no table is used; if time and space are dedicated to respectfully listening to the words spoken and feelings expressed, a Circle has been convened. The use of a talking piece—an elk tooth keychain, a ball of yarn, or a stone—can always be helpful in defining the process as sacred.

8

How the Circle Process Works

GARFIELD, SPRING, AND CAHILL aptly capture the precepts of the Circle process:

- Honor the Circle as sacred time and space by using simple rituals to mark the opening and closing.

- Create a collective center by mutually agreeing on a topic or intention.

- Ask to be informed by our highest human values such as compassion and truth, by the wisdom of our ancestors, and by the needs of those yet to be born.

- Express gratitude and heartfelt appreciation for the blessings and teachings of life.

- Create a safe container for full participation and deep truth-telling.

- Listen from the heart, and serve as a compassionate witness for the other people in the Circle.

- Speak from the heart and from direct experience.

- Make room for silence to enter.

- Empower each member to be a co-facilitator of the process.

- Commit to an ongoing relationship with the people in the group, and carry the intentions of the Circle into daily life.[1]

---

1. Garfield et al., *Wisdom Circles*, 16.

Ball, Caldwell, and Pranis;[2] Pranis;[3] Ross;[4] and Stuart[5] have described the key elements of Circle processes. Below I will revisit these elements and elaborate on them in light of our experience in the Community Circles program. It is important to understand that the Circle process is not static, and that it should be considered adaptable to different cultures, new situations, and new challenges.

The Circle Format

Participants are seated in a Circle, with or without chairs, and with no table or other obstruction blocking sight and sound lines. A flower, a lighted candle, or other object(s) familiar to or valued by participants is sometimes placed in the center of the Circle to focus the group on the purpose for which the Circle has been convened.

In Community Circles, rather than distributing pads, pens, water, or tissues to participants—with the assumption that they will need or want them—these items are placed in the center of the Circle. If a person is obviously in need of a tissue, *any* Circle member can hand it to them—emphasizing shared responsibility. To ensure that participants will be able to listen intently to the words spoken by others, pads and pens allow people to make quick notes in preparation for their turn to speak, and to then immediately return their focus to the stories being voiced by others.

In Circles, all participants are equal, all share leadership, and all share responsibility for upholding the tenets and maintaining the guidelines (see below) of the process. The equality of participants deserves a further note. Sometimes, Circles include people of vastly different economic means, with different levels of education, and with different professional titles and implied levels of status. Such hierarchical rankings are meaningful to some participants as key components of their identities, and the importance of those identity issues must be understood and acknowledged by the Circle Keepers. It may be difficult for participants with strong identity issues to initially embrace the Circle process. One participant in a Community Circles training seminar said that the most challenging thing for her to do was to step back from her professional position as a supervisor and

2. Ball et al., *Doing Democracy with Circles.*

3. Pranis, *Little Book of Circle Processes.*

4. Ross, *Dancing with a Ghost.*

5. Stuart, *Building Community Justice Partnerships.*

decision-maker, and acknowledge the value of the contributions of *all* of the Circle members.

In Community Circles, we suggest that each guest (the person for whom the Circle has been convened) bring one or more supporters to the Circle—a family member, coach, friend, counselor, or advisor. Supporters are important for the restorative journey ahead, and if one of our guests has no supporters—and this is not unusual—the Circle Keepers become the guest's supporters. We have learned that regardless of how valuable it might be to have an officer of the court (juvenile probation office or other) participate in Circles referred by a court, the confidentiality mandate (see below) of the Circle process precludes their participation.

A great benefit of the Circle process is the fact that everyone can see and feel the emotions of the participants, evidenced not only by their words, but also by their facial expressions and their kinesics. I have become aware of how beneficial the Circle process *could* be in many community meetings—as I stare at the backs of the heads of people in the row ahead of me.

Talking Piece

A talking piece can be a key to successful Circle processes, its purpose being to manage the conversation between the participants. Only the person holding the talking piece has the permission of the group to speak. Each participant in the Circle knows that they will also be listened to intently when they hold the talking piece and have the opportunity to speak—to tell their story.

In Community Circles, we invite each guest to bring an item of significance with them to use as a talking piece; and guests have brought such items as a small clay statue, a picture of an estranged loved one, a weathered stick, and various handmade art objects—including a horsehair-braided belt buckle made during a period of incarceration. One guest presented Community Circles with a handcrafted, beaded stick as a token of his appreciation, and it continues to be a treasured part of our culture. Using an item of significance to the guest relieves their anxiety, and lets them know that they are valued as a human being.

In the Community Circles program, we place a glass bowl containing rounded, naturally colored stones in the center of the Circle, with each stone having engraved on it a single word—such as Peace, Wisdom, Hope, Courage, Love, Joy, Believe, Creativity, Trust, Dream, or Healing. If a guest chooses to use one of the colored stones as a talking piece, we then have an opportunity to use their choice, if appropriate, to open a door for them to tell their story. At the concluding Circle meeting with a guest, we offer them the stone that they have chosen, as a gift and remembrance of their Circle experience.

Traditionally, in many indigenous cultures, the talking piece moves clockwise, and is passed from person to adjacent person. I participated in a week-long Circle process training seminar several years ago with Phillip Gatensby, a Tlingit tribal member. After holding the talking piece and speaking, I decided to pass it to another trainee across the Circle who seemed about to explode with a need to speak. I was then gently reminded by Phillip that it was proper, at least in the Tlingit culture, for the talking piece to pass only to the adjacent person in the Circle.

In Community Circles, we honor the above tradition, and have also learned that in some circumstances a degree of process flexibility can work well. If two individuals—such as a parent and a teenager, or a harmed person and the one who caused the harm—are engaged in a productive dialogue, rather than repeatedly passing the talking piece around the Circle, it can be effective to allow it to pass directly between the engaged parties. This is a strategic decision by the Circle Keepers. If, during such a change from the traditional process, a conversation becomes heated, or if several people start to talk at once, the clockwise rotation can be reintroduced by the Circle Keepers. This, again, is a strategic decision, and one that invariably restores participants to respectful and thoughtful speaking and listening. If, at the close of a Circle, participants want to discuss together what has just happened, a Circle Keeper can place the talking piece in the center of the Circle and indicate that a free-form discussion among all participants is supported.

My seven-year-old grandson, during a tiff with his younger sister, grabbed a stuffed alligator toy and said, "Mom, this is going to be our talking piece."

Circle Process Guidelines

Circle Keepers have an opportunity at the beginning of each Circle to emphasize the purpose for which the Circle has been convened, to suggest that first names be used (with nametags if appropriate), and to talk about the role of the talking piece. Although group guidelines can vary, some that have worked well in Community Circles are as follows:

- Personal information shared in Circles is kept confidential, except when issues of safety or legality are involved (see further discussion below).
- Participants agree to honor the talking piece.
- Participants can pass the talking piece without speaking.
- Participants agree to speak with respect, in a good way.
- Participants agree to speak from their hearts.
- Participants agree to speak only for themselves and not for others or for a group.
- Participants agree to honor the need for everyone to have time to tell their story.
- Participants agree to listen intently to the words spoken and the feelings expressed.
- Participants agree to allow the outward display of emotions, and to be present for Circle members who are in need of support.
- Participants agree not to call down or judge others, and to build only on positive points raised by them.
- Participants agree to strive for cooperative interactions between Circle members.
- Participants agree to stay in the Circle until everyone agrees to bring it to a close.
- Participants agree to support the decision-making process agreed on by the group, if decisions are the stated goal of the Circle (see further discussion below).

Several other guidelines that might be appropriate, depending on circumstances, include: (1) no cell phones, (2) no interrupting, (3) no character attacks, (4) speaking for no more than two minutes at a time, and (5) no weapons.

Rather than imposing guidelines on Circle participants, Circle Keepers might suggest that the ones listed above (either handed out in written form or verbalized) are some that other Circle participants have found to be useful. They can then ask: "Is there anyone who cannot agree to the guidelines?" "Are there any other guidelines you would like to have in place?" When participants have agreed on guidelines, realize that the group has reached its first agreement. Depending on circumstances, you might mention this fact to the group, or just keep it to yourself. With group guidelines in place, Circle Keepers can always refresh participants' memories if such becomes necessary.

Opening the Circle

It is important to define the Circle as a special time and space. In Community Circles, we call it a sacred time and a sacred space—revered, respected, protected, and secure. Some participants consider the Circle to be a spiritual time and space, but this is a determination reserved to each participant. We feel that it is important to specifically mention the definition of "sacred," and to dedicate sufficient time to Circle openings. Otherwise there is a risk that the Circle might lapse into a mere geometric format for holding a meeting.

In some Circle programs, the person for whom the Circle has been convened is given the option of opening the Circle. This invitation can be a way of honoring the guest, and letting them know that they are valued as a member of the Circle.

> Those who come to the meeting focused upon individual agendas as opposed to common, larger goals will, consciously or not, put up roadblocks, if only by sending signals of antagonism or defensiveness. By contrast, this simple reminder of the good that is in each of us, of the good that we can each contribute and of the good fortune that surrounds us, prompts real effort at patience, understanding and cooperation.[6]

Music can be played to open a Circle if such is appropriate and meets the desires or expectations of the group. A prayer can also be offered if appropriate, and if all participants agree. Openings can include short sayings or poems, reflective thoughts about connectedness or purpose, or a short period of silence. Some cultures burn sage or sweetgrass and smudge each participant with it to open the Circle. Smudging with sage was used to open

6. Ross, *Dancing with a Ghost*, 40.

the Circles in the training seminar I attended with Phillip Gatensby. The opening of the Circle should not reflect any particular religious belief (unless appropriate), but rather should provide a tranquil time for participants to focus on the purpose for which the Circle has been convened.

In Community Circles, we open Circles with a period of silence, during which time participants can close their eyes if they so wish and if they feel comfortable in so doing. Many years ago, it was brought to my attention that bad memories might be associated with closing one's eyes, so it is important to stress that it is just an option. It is also important to let people know the approximate length of the period of silence and how it will be ended—e.g., two minutes, with a bell, or with the word "set"—so that participants can focus on achieving inner calm rather than on the duration of the silence.

Check-In Circle

I cannot overemphasize the importance of the check-in Circle. For a person to listen intently to others, they must first be listened to and have their feelings acknowledged. In our Western culture, we often begin business and community meetings with an agenda in hand, and with an all-important linear timeline to adhere to—for the sake of speed and efficiency. Group time is, indeed, valuable and we should honor it, but if we do not know *whom* each person has brought to the meeting, group time is squandered.

If a person has just caught the trout of a lifetime, they will not have their mind or heart within the Circle or at the meeting until they have had a chance to talk about it. And if another person has just received a serious medical diagnosis or admitted a family member to the hospital, the Circle or the meeting will be unproductive until the emotions of that person have been acknowledged. People are not present until they have had a chance to tell others *whom* they have brought to the gathering. This is a simple yet extremely important concept, and an important investment of time that applies to all Circles, whether with family members or with corporate board members.

At a recent Circle Keeper training seminar for female staff members of a residential youth facility, I began the day with a check-in Circle. Things not previously revealed to fellow workers included, among others, a declaration by a husband the night before that he was going to file for divorce, and a recent diagnosis of cancer. These people now felt listened to. A woman whose husband had just retired shared the most memorable story. She burst into tears and related that her husband was going to fulfill his lifelong dream of buying a motorcycle and riding it to Las Vegas. This was well enough, except for the fact that he expected her to ride behind him—and she was terrified.

Closing the Circle

Circles can be closed effectively by passing the talking piece around the Circle a final time and asking participants, if they so choose, to share their feelings about what they have experienced. After the talking piece returns to one of the Circles Keepers, we have found that a period of silence provides a meaningful transition from the calm and closeness of the Circle to the bustle of the world outside the Circle—including such tasks as picking kids up from dance lessons, preparing meals, or worrying about that new and strange noise coming from your car's engine. If Circle participants immediately engage in conversation following the last rotation of the talking piece, rather than imposing a period of silence, Circle Keepers might consider it more appropriate to join in the conversation—even to voice a request for advice regarding that strange new sound coming from *their* car's engine. At the risk of being repetitive, many decisions by Circle Keepers are strategic ones, and are always within the context of the purpose for which the Circle has been convened.

Who Can Convene a Circle?

There are no rules about who can convene a Circle, although existing family, neighborhood, civic, or business commitments might dictate scheduling. People who ask to convene a Circle do so out of a need to say something and be listened to, and that need must be accommodated. Invited participants must be vigilant about learning the nature of the issue and its time sensitivity, so that the needs of the person requesting the Circle can be met. If preliminary fact-finding is to be conducted, sufficient time must be allowed, and the means for doing so must be determined.

It is understood that, in many organizational cultures, the idea that an employee has the right to convene a Circle is outside the bounds of protocol. In these cases, a change in the culture could only enhance interpersonal relationships and the opportunity for success.

Circle Guidance Strategies

Strategies evolve and become a part of the culture of all Circle programs. One overarching strategy to keep in mind, in Circles of all types and sizes, is to look for opportunities to give energy to other Circle participants whenever possible. Relationships change with each interaction; with each interaction there is the opportunity to either give energy or to take it away. One good way to give energy to the person for whom the Circle has been convened is to invite them to use a talking piece of their choosing; another way is to acknowledge their possible anxiety at the beginning of the Circle. The simple step of asking the first-arriving participant to help set up chairs, and the second-arriving person to distribute nametags, gives people a sense of inclusion in the Circle process. A valuable overarching strategy is to trust the process. You will easily be able to add to this list. Rather than considering the above strategies to be platitudes, look at them as rock-solid principles for Circles involving two to twenty participants.

Some other strategies that have proven useful in the Community Circles program are:

- Have each potential guest complete an application form, on which two of the key questions are: "Do you want to move forward onto a better life path?" and "What do you plan to do to make that happen?"

- An initial meeting with each of the guests assures the Circle Keepers that the guests understand the Circle process and are willing to participate in good faith, including physically showing up and abiding by Circle guidelines.

- Always have at least two trained Circle Keepers in each Circle.

- The meeting space for Circles must be comfortable and safe, and the following factors should be considered:

  - A quiet space without undue road or hall noise or other interruptions,

  - A confidential space,

  - Accommodations for special needs,

  - An appropriate number of comfortable chairs,

  - Adequate lighting and temperature controls,

  - Access to restrooms.

- Confirm the Circle location, date, and time with all participants.

- Provide nametags, pads, pens, liquid refreshments, tissues, talking pieces, and other supplies.

- Prepare the meeting space, including having no extra chairs in the Circle unless an empty chair honors a previous participant who is not able to attend.

- Meet with your fellow Circle Keeper(s) before the planned Circle to review notes from previous Circles, and to consider what might go wrong.

- Greet all participants.

- Introduce yourselves and have all participants introduce themselves.

- Address logistical matters, such as the location of restrooms and procedures for calling for "breaks."

- Explain the purpose of the Circle (be clear about why the Circle has been convened, whether it is to discuss a specific incident, share views about a potential problem or a pending decision, or for some other purpose).

- Give participants an opportunity to voice the values that they feel should guide the Circle.

- Discuss guidelines for Circle participation.

- Explain the use of the talking piece and designate the talking piece to be used.

- Suggest that the Circle continue for a set period of time—e.g., two hours—and that the group will then take a break and decide whether to continue or to conclude for the day and schedule another Circle.

- Open the Circle using a prayer, a reading, silence, or some other means of defining the Circle as a sacred time and space.

- Be aware of the three types of conversations: (1) what happened, (2) my feelings, and (3) my identity—how I want to be viewed by others.

- Understand and be aware of participants' conflict styles: (1) competition, (2) avoidance, (3) accommodation, (4) or collaboration.

- Summarize information as appropriate.

- Clarify unresolved issues for the purpose of focusing the Circle's energy.

- Guide the search for common understanding.

- Give participants ample time to tell their stories.

- Shape conversations into consideration of past events (commonly negative), current Circle participation (positive), and future possibilities (hopeful).

- Guide participants to move from the old conversation of blame, recrimination, judgment, and victimization to a new conversation of honesty, openness, compassion, empathy, hope and possibilities.

- Guide participants to move from debate to dialogue, blame to understanding, certainty to curiosity, and from the use of labels to the acknowledgment of participants as individuals.

- Help the group search for options.

- Assist the group in reaching a decision, if such is the goal.

- Be certain that agreed-upon plans are measureable—with established timelines.

- Help the participants solidify their plans: what will be done, how will it be accomplished and by whom, and when will it be completed.

- Ensure that all participants are clear about the next step in the process—e.g., another Circle (location, date, time)—and about their responsibilities between now and the next event.

- Pick up and move forward from setbacks.

- Celebrate success.

- Close the Circle in an appropriate manner.

- Act as timekeeper for the group.

- Hold a debrief meeting with Circle Keepers.

- Honor the process at all times.

- Trust the process at all times.

- Do no harm.

It is important to be aware of and to acknowledge guests' cultures, and to choose Circle Keepers accordingly, if appropriate. As Circle Keepers, we may normally think of cultural issues in terms of such obvious attributes as ethnicity or race.

Rupert Ross, a Crown attorney, relates his initial difficulty in understanding the unwillingness of Ojibway and Cree tribal members to give advice, cast blame, burden people with their individual problems, or to interfere in the lives of others—all cultural values that were critical to communal survival during hunting and gathering activities.[7]

Intent listening is a vital tool for learning about and appreciating cultures different from our own. Cultural factors within our own communities that are worthy of consideration are: economic situations different from our own, reading and/or writing skills different from our own, and religious beliefs and practices different from our own. Giving careful consideration to cultural issues will allow us to guide Circles effectively on behalf of our guests.

Circle Keeper Strategies

> [It is] a very great art to talk eloquently and well, but an equally great one to know the right moment to stop.[8]

Because we guide rather than lead, and because we engage in exploration with each Circle, it is important that Circle Keepers listen carefully, offer comments thoughtfully, and remain constantly aware of the needs of the parties. We enter each Circle armed only with a strong commitment to the integrity of and respect for the principles of restorative justice. Some strategies that have proven useful in the Community Circles program are listed below:

- Acknowledge your own health, emotions, and capabilities; care for yourself.
- Before Circles, take time to establish inner calm.
- Think clearly about what you know (your feelings, experiences, identity issues) and what you don't know (guests' feelings, intentions, perspectives).
- Be aware of your own assumptions.

7. Ross, *Dancing with a Ghost*.
8. Mozart, *Letters*, 233.

- Be aware of your biases regarding participants, based on such things as appearance and speech patterns. Enact what I call "operational impartiality."

- Provide a safe and respectful space in which difficult issues can be discussed.

- Acknowledge the feelings of participants.

- Validate by listening; listening is an active step.

- Listen for unexpressed emotions.

- Resist the urge to counsel or to solve problems; Circle Keepers are not interventionists.

- Do not try to change other people.

- Keep "our stuff" separate from "their stuff."

- Use an encouraging, calm tone of voice.

- Create a tone of hope and optimism.

- Be careful about word choice, including joking and informal comments.

- Always speak from your heart.

- Model the use of "I" statements, if culturally appropriate.

- Be aware of your facial expressions and body language.

- Consider yourself to be a servant to the group.

- Consider your gift to be "caring."

- Reframe issues as appropriate—e.g., "What do you plan to do?" versus "What would you like to have happen"?

- Help participants to refocus, if necessary, on the issues for which the Circle has been convened.

- Normalize discussion issues, if appropriate.

- Mutualize discussion issues, if appropriate.

- Remind participants of the guidelines, if appropriate.

- Summarize points raised in the conversation, if appropriate.

- Be aware of "presenting (substantive) issues," with the understanding that they are underlain by both relationship and identity issues.

- Be aware of the importance of identity; help people save face.

- Be aware that nobody likes to be demeaned in any way.

- Be aware that all people want three things: (1) attention, (2) acceptance, and (3) appreciation.

- Be aware that anger is a secondary emotion; search for the cause.

- Follow rather than lead; be a guide on a journey of discovery rather than a leader on a well-trodden trail.

- Focus on the now; be in the present; leave outside concerns, issues, etc. outside the Circle.

- Acknowledge the legitimacy of speakers' emotions.

- Share personal stories if you feel that they will offer positive guidance to the parties.

- Use questions rather than statements whenever possible—especially when statements are actually furtive judgment or advice.

- Listen for judgmental words and phrases, and identify them to the participants. It may be valuable to point out that implied judgmental words like "should" and "should have" are equally as damaging as overtly judgmental words.

- Be a compassionate listener; storytelling is a tool for developing relationships.

- Participate as a community member.

- Look for opportunities to give energy to other Circle participants—e.g., consider giving everyone in the Circle an opportunity to say something *positive* about the person for whom the Circle has been convened.

- Be aware of the needs of all Circle participants—from bathroom breaks to emotional time-outs.

- Slow things down if, strategically, you feel that it might calm nerves, offer relaxation, or allow good thought time.

- Do not be afraid of silence. Honor it and develop comfort with it. Silence is an action step, not dead air. What follows a period of silence are usually well-thought-out words. Listening is the key to connecting.

- Count to ten before responding after an expression of strong emotions.

- Be honest, but talk with the intention of helping to improve the situation.

A further word about assumptions is warranted. I recall that at the start of a mediation conference one of the parties was tense, fidgety, red-faced, sweating, and seemingly ready to explode. I was concerned, and made mental and physical safety preparations for the anticipated outburst. When the time came for him to speak, he broke down in tears and, in a whimper, told how he was devastated about being falsely accused of a negative act.

Consider seating people in the Circle strategically. If a Circle Keeper would like a particular person to be the first recipient of the talking piece, suggest that that person sit to the Circle Keeper's immediate left. If a guest's supporter is present, perhaps the guest would be comfortable having that person close by. And if a victim and an offender are both present, seating them on opposite sides of the Circle might be appropriate. Circle Keepers are most effective when seated across from each other so that strategic actions, such as calling for a break, can be managed in a timely manner. It is important to always accede to the needs and desires of the Circle participants. Remember, at all times, that we are the guides and the servants of the participants.

We have found that it is important to hold a debrief meeting following each Circle, and to write up notes about the events that took place, commitments that were made, and impressions that Circle Keepers had. Circle Keeper notes can be sent by email to one of the Circles Keepers for compilation following the Circle, or one of the Circle Keepers can solely write up the notes. The notes should capture the essence of the Circle, responsibilities agreed upon by the parties, topics to be addressed in the next Circle, and the date and time for the next Circle. The notes are reviewed by the Circle Keepers just before the start of the next Circle.

Circle Keeper Qualities

A word that aptly defines a good quality for Circle Keepers to have is the Greek-based word "autotelic"—"having a purpose in and not apart from itself."[9] With that definition in mind, a Circle Keeper should participate out of a sincere desire to help individuals move to better life paths, and to help groups resolve problems and design good futures. People should not participate in the Circle process for an ulterior purpose such as making money.

9. *New Oxford American Dictionary.*

Many of the people we have as guests in Circles have broken laws or community expectations, and some may have a deficiency in education, mental capacity, or self-respect. Patience and compassion, therefore, are two of the more important qualities for Circle Keepers to have. Empathy, good listening skills, and the ability to honor silence are also important qualities.

Finally, quoting Cicero:

Silence is one of the great arts of conversation.[10]

The Importance of Stories

Recall the last time someone asked you a question, and then waited patiently and attentively while you answered it. How did it feel? Yes, it felt good! You sensed that the questioner cared about listening to your words, and was focused on understanding the feelings within your words. Think back to the questioner's rapt attention, and your sense that a precious gift had been transferred from one human being to another.

Telling and listening to stories comprise those special times when people invest in each other's lives—regardless of whether the stories relate fear, pain, grief, agony, disappointment, challenge, achievement, forgiveness, joy, or hope. The time and the space in which people share stories—in which they feel comfortable talking about things of importance to them—is sacred, and the Circle process is a proven way of providing that time and space. Stories define the world in which people have lived, in which they now live, and the world in which they hope to live in the future. Stories can bring to the surface boundaries that have manacled emotions, such as fear, regret, and animosity. Storytelling can be a tool for breaking down those boundaries, and for moving people forward toward healthier relationships. Being able to tell one's story—uninterrupted and without judgment— brings a sense of relief to the storyteller—a release of emotions long hidden, buried, unexpressed. Compassionate listening is a gift, and providing time and space for storytelling is very important.

Passing cultural information (memes) from generation to generation in Circles has been a keystone in providing for safety, security, health, and fulfillment in tribal communities for thousands of years. Memes passed to me by my grandparents, my father, and my mother—commonly around a dining table or a campfire—comprise the wisdom that has allowed me to make sense

10. Quoted in More, *Works of Hannah More*, 555.

of the facts, the happenings, the relationships, and the knowledge in our ever more complex world. A valuable consideration to ponder is whether cultural wisdom can be effectively transferred *without* face-to-face storytelling.

The following description of events in a meeting of Natives in Northern Ontario highlights the importance of storytelling:

> The chairman will never say "Gentlemen, give me your recommendations," and none of the others will say "I think we should do this, and here are my reasons." Instead, everyone takes turns making speeches, which recite facts but seem to contain no opinions. One speech follows another, with none of the frequent give-and-take which constitutes a discussion for us. The speeches seem to go in circles, with many things being repeated by each speaker, often more than once. No one seems to venture a recommendation or state a point of view. In fact, meetings often seem to end this way, with no apparent conclusion having been reached at all.
>
> The strange thing is that the participants usually agree that a conclusion *has* been reached. . . . It is as if a common agreement on the pertinent facts which drive a particular conclusion is all that's necessary. The conclusion itself need not even be articulated; everyone goes away knowing what it is. . . .
>
> It is this sort of ordering of relevant facts, this sort of sifting to shake out the truly significant facts, which I sense governs group decision-making among Native people. The meeting ends and the decision, though perhaps never articulated, is agreeable to all. In this way it becomes a group decision. Most importantly, it is arrived at without anyone "losing," without anyone having his or her opinion ignored or discounted.[11]

The movie *Twelve Angry Men* serves as a good example of the value of providing time and space for people to tell their stories. With Henry Fonda's strong yet compassionate guidance during jury deliberations in a murder trial, the jurors moved from voting "guilty," with one "not certain," to twelve members voting for "acquittal." The time taken to carefully review all aspects of the evidence, and to hear the personal stories of the twelve jurors, was critical to the group reaching its decision. Although the table was rectangular instead of circular, the time and space dedicated to hearing all opinions and concerns was a key reason that the group was able to reach a decision to which all members could subscribe.

---

11. Ross, *Dancing with a Ghost*, 22–23.

Stories hold the power to help people move beyond the negative and often destructive tale of the past, to write an optimistic story of the future, and to define a strategy for success. Stories define a person's needs, desires, and dreams and, by the repeated sharing of their personal story with others, tellers are able to better calibrate their life events with those of their community. We, as Circle Keepers, are respectful visitors in the stories of our guests.

Stories of the Past

Cloke and Goldsmith[12] have a keen awareness of the importance of external and internal stories, and of the challenge to Circle Keepers of listening closely to them. Although stories can be told in writing (prose, poetry, journalizing) or in art (painting, sculpture, dance), the verbal telling of stories is the form that most meaningfully meshes with the Circle process.

External stories are those that people tell to blame others for causing them pain, and such stories usually focus on actions that took place in the past. External stories are the storyteller's view of the truth—even though words conveying negative images might have been removed, and words enhancing positive images might have been added. External stories build defenses to protect the storyteller, often include judgmental statements, and are often used to garner support. It is important to acknowledge that all stories are true to the teller—perhaps not factually, but at least metaphorically. Circle Keepers listen to external stories and strive to understand them by putting a context on the metaphors employed, and by gauging the facial expressions and kinesics of the speaker.

Internal stories are those that people tell themselves to justify who they are, to cement their identities, to solidify their worldview, to emphasize their innocence, to lessen their suffering, and to help them find voice. Again, these stories are the storyteller's view of the truth and may include an enhancement or diminishment of reality. Cloke and Goldsmith introduce the notion of the "core story"[13]—the real story that is masked by the external and internal one. The core story neutralizes accusations, questions excuses, accepts responsibility, acknowledges a willingness to learn, and converges both external and internal stories toward a valuable

---

12. Cloke and Goldsmith, *Resolving Personal and Organizational Conflict*.
13. Ibid.

growth experience. Core stories, once revealed, can provide an opportunity for forgiveness and reconciliation.

Only after a person has had a chance to tell their story, and has had their story listened to and acknowledged by the participants in the Circle, can they move beyond their story of the past, toward a more positive story of the future.

The charge of Circle Keepers is a daunting one: to listen attentively and compassionately to the words spoken, including the metaphors, and to then guide parties to discover their core stories and to build their future on those stories in a good way. We may want desperately to push our guests toward a better life path, but that is not our job. Circle Keepers do not have to use blind faith or to accept a storyteller's tale. The Circle process allows Circle Keepers to ask questions that will let them evaluate the verity of words spoken and, through visual observation, the verity of the words unspoken and the feelings not verbalized. Questions are valuable, and will be addressed further in the next section. For now, let's consider a few questions that will set the tone for the Circle Keeper's task: (1) Why are they telling their story? (2) What need is being fulfilled by them telling their story? (3) What is true about their story? (4) What have they learned from their story? (5) What would happen if their story ended with "and they lived happily ever after"? (6) Did they ever have a story in which people did live happily ever after? (7) What made it possible? Circle Keepers can use these questions to guide guests to transform their core stories into strategies for success—whether the guest is an individual or a group of individuals.

It is true that stories of the past can sometimes be used to manipulate or to garner support, so a check for congruency between the tone and intensity of the words spoken, facial expressions, and kinesics is critical. Note that without face-to-face meetings such a check for congruency would not be possible. This is yet another benefit of the Circle process.

Stories of the Future

Stories can focus very beneficially on the future—on gifts that people are eager to share, on opportunities that can be seized, and on plans that can be implemented. Stories of the future can bring new ideas to the surface, and can awaken latent talents, inspirations, and glimpses of wisdom. The guiding role of the Circle Keeper is nowhere of greater importance than in helping guests focus on their assets, and helping them design a positive future of their choice.

The Value of Questions

Questions are gifts we give to people we care about.[14]

A question not asked is a door not opened.[15]

The big question is whether you are going to be able to say a hearty yes to your adventure.[16]

It is important to be aware of the role that answers play in our lives, and in the lives of our guests—with answers being a comforting attachment to knowing and an avoidance of the anxiety associated with not knowing—or appearing not to know. Yet it is questions that can lead to new pathways, experiences, opportunities, explorations, directions, and possibly better answers to existing questions—and even to the generation of new and exciting ones. Questions play a fundamental role in the creative process. They elicit curiosity, and evidence a desire to learn. Despite the presence of questions in our lives every day, few people take the time to acknowledge their potential. Solutions to problems might remain forever behind closed doors, unless those doors are opened by the right questions.

Healthy interpersonal communication is a conversational dance of questions and statements, but much of what we, as Circle Keepers, hear in Circles is only the statement part of the dance—the declarations and assertions about what is going on, the "presenting issues." Such declarations and assertions preclude the exploration of relationship and identity issues. They eliminate an acknowledgment that change is possible, and that the future can be different from, and better than, the past. One of our roles as Circle Keepers is to help our guests learn to ask their own questions—ones that can herald their own positive futures. As Circle Keepers, we can use questions to good benefit, but (1) we should always keep in mind that questions answerable by either "yes" or "no" lead to blind alleys, and (2) we should never *require* an answer.

14 Lavery, personal communication with author.

15. Goldberg, *Art of the Question*, ix.

16. Joseph Campbell, http://www.brainyquote.com/quotes/quotes/j/josephcamp 157106.html.

Marilee Goldberg[17] and the staff of the Public Conversations Project[18] have catalogued six types of questions, and offer suggestions for their use. The questions shown below are ones that we might ask when serving as Community Circles Circle Keepers.

External and Internal Questions

When we conduct pre-Circle orientation meetings, we ask external questions of our guests, for example:

- Have you read the information we sent you about Community Circles?
- Do you understand the purpose of Community Circles, and agree to act in accordance with its purpose?
- Do you agree to the requirements for participation in the Community Circles program?
- Do you understand the limits of confidentiality of the Circle process?
- Do you have supporters who are willing and committed to going on this journey with you?
- How do you feel the Circle process can help you?
- What are your expectations?
- Whom do you feel has been harmed?
- Do you want to move forward onto a better life path?
- Have you begun making better choices? What are they?
- What steps are you willing to take to make things better?
- What steps are you willing to take in order to improve the situation for your family and the community?
- What's going on?

One reason for asking the above external questions is to answer our own internal ones, for example:

- What will this person be like?
- What problems will be presented?

17. Goldberg, *Art of the Question.*
18. Public Conversations Project training manual.

- What information will be withheld?
- Will there be a hidden agenda?
- How much rigidity, defensiveness, resistance, or hostility will be evident?
- What are this person's needs?
- How can we best help this individual?
- What might go wrong?

During Circles, our internal questions continue:

- Why is this person telling me this?
- What about their story is true, is designed to focus blame on others, or is being told to relieve self-suffering?
- What's the most helpful thing to do now?
- Should I ask another question?
- Should I be silent to let them absorb what just happened?
- How much wait-time should I allow before I speak?
- What role should I assume now—supporter, educator, focuser, challenger?
- What are the dynamics between the group members?
- Who is trying to control the meeting?
- Who are the silent members?
- When should I advise the group about timing?
- How might he react if I mentioned his loud toe-tapping?

It's important to realize that, at the same time we are asking questions, our guests are asking their own internal questions and trying to find answers to them. Our responsibility, as Circle Keepers, is to listen carefully to our guests' external stories and, with questions, elicit information on their core stories. By continually checking for congruence between words, facial expressions, and kinesics, we will be able to guide them toward a better path.

Problem-Focused and Solution-Focused Questions

Internal, problem-focused questions pondered by guests presuppose that things were bad, painful, and undesirable in the past, that they are the same now, and that they will continue to be the same in the future. In light of these negative questions, future possibilities are seriously limited. Examples of guests' internal, problem-focused questions might include:

- Why am I such a failure?
- Why don't the breaks come my way?
- Why do I have all the bad luck?
- Why should I try?—because there's really no way out.
- Why can't our group ever seem to work well together?

Circle Keepers, intuiting that guests are stuck asking problem-focused questions, can offer acknowledgment, and then guide them toward a more fertile field of possibilities.

Solution-focused questions pondered by guests presuppose that whatever was the case in the past can be relegated to the past and left there to be appreciated and learned from, and that the future can be different from the past. Options, especially positive ones, are possible. Examples of guests' internal, solution-focused questions might include:

- What can I do?
- What can I learn from this?
- In what way might this be useful?
- What are my possibilities?
- How can I take advantage of this opportunity?

Circle Keepers can listen for positive questions verbalized by guests, and build on them.

Judgment and Learning Questions

Internal, judgment questions pondered by guests are inflexible and oriented to the past. They reflect a world that is black or white, good or bad, right or wrong. Such questions might include:

- Who is wrong?

- Who is to blame?

- How can I protect myself?

- What arguments would help me win?

- How can I prove my point?

- Why does this always happen to me?

Learning questions pondered by guests are open-minded, future-oriented, and accepting of themselves and others. They envision a world that is not good or bad, right or wrong, black or white, but rather one that has many shades of gray and the potential to be brightly colored. Internal learning questions by guests might include:

- What's going on here?

- What can I learn from this?

- What's useful or valuable about this?

- Do I want it hard enough to work at it?

- Am I still on the right path?

- What patterns exist that might lead to greater understanding?

- What's the best thing to do now?

- Are we moving in a helpful direction?

- How can we resolve this to our mutual satisfaction?

Again, Circle Keepers can listen for learning questions verbalized by guests, and build on them. Examples of learning questions that might be voiced by Circle Keepers include:[19]

- What are your strengths?

- What are some of your recent accomplishments?

- What special talents (gifts) can you offer to your family and the community?

- What are you grateful for that you've never spoken about?

- When have you faced a situation with similar features in the past, and things worked out well?

19 These questions are modified from ibid.

- What did you do, think, or feel that allowed things to go successfully?

- Have there been times when someone has given you the message that your efforts on this challenge have been appreciated? What did you learn about your capacities through their appreciation?

- Is there someone you deeply respect whose wisdom might be helpful right now? What advice might they give you? What qualities or abilities would they see in you that they might encourage you to call on?

- Have there been times in this or a similar situation when you felt that you were being the very best you, even for a brief period of time? What made that possible? How did that feel?

- How do you imagine you might make use of what you most value in this situation?

- Have there been times when you've felt you've been working shoulder to shoulder with others who are involved in this situation? How did that feel?

- What stands out in your mind about that effort? What enabled you to work together?

- What would you say to someone if you could let your guard down completely, vent, get everything off your chest—all without negative consequences? How did it make you feel?

Some Ways in Which We Can Use Questions:

- Reframing:

   If you would only do your share of the work around
   here, we'd be finished by noon.

   So, you'd like to get out of here early and would like more
   help. Is that right?

- Normalization:

   I know of other people in similar situations who have
   been able to reach satisfactory solutions to these very
   challenging issues, in a reasonable amount of time.
   Would you like to continue?

- Mutualization:

It seems like the only way to solve the situation is to have you combine your efforts. Why would you want to attack the person who holds the key to getting what you want?

- Role reversal:

    If you were in John's position, what would you see as a reasonable solution?

- Dissociation:

    In time -

    If, two years from now, you look at what you've accomplished today and it's a work of art, what are the first two things you think of?

    In place -

    When you go to a balcony and view the proceedings, how do you feel about them?

    In person -

    If you advertise your agreement to your family and friends, would they see it as fair?

    In time, place, and person -

    Imagine your children are now grown, live in another town, and look back at what you've accomplished today. How would they feel about it?

- What if?:

    If you get everything you want, which of your life needs would be fulfilled?

- Doubt and dissonance:

    I don't expect you to agree with anything I'm going to say, but if you do, please let me know, okay?

What's your best alternative to a negotiated agreement (BATNA)?[20]

What do you see as the strengths of your case?

What do you see as the weaknesses of your case?

What do you see as the strengths of the other party's case?

How do you think a judge would view this situation?

How do you think the other party would answer these questions?

- Clarifying communications:

  Can you help me understand how you reached that conclusion?

  What experience have you had that has led you to feel this way?

  Can you tell me more about that?

  Let me tell you what I'm hearing you say . . . Is that right?

  What I understand is . . . is that right?

- Clarifying, verifying, empathizing, problem-solving:

  What part of the problem is most important to you right now?

  Who are the people most immediately involved?

  Whom could we go talk to about this?

  Maybe we'll have to go to that, but let's see what we might try first. Is that okay?

  I want to hear more about your objections. Please tell me, what is not working for you?

  I understand how you're feeling, but you know I can't do what you are asking. That approach would violate what I hold most dear. What makes that decision your first choice?

20. Fisher and Ury, *Getting to Yes.*

83

Using Questions for Giving Energy to Circle Guests

- What are your feelings regarding the situation?

- What would you like to get clear about today?

- What is the goal you would like to achieve?

- What solutions have you attempted so far? What was it about these attempts that worked or didn't work?

- What does a good outcome look like to you?

- What are you going to do to make it happen? (In contrast to the more frequently posed question: What would you like to have happen?)

- What I hear you saying is . . . is that right?

Clarifying information by using the three words "is that right?" not only ensures that the conversation is on track, but it is also an easy and important way in which to give energy to our guests.

Some New Ways in Which to Think about Questions:

- Questions are pokes and prods at those things that have not yet been poked and prodded.

- Questions are invitations to creativity.

- Questions are beginnings to adventures.

- Questions are unsettled and unsettling issues.

- Questions are disguised answers.

- Questions are points of departure.

- Questions have no ends and no beginnings.

- Questions are a smorgasbord offered to a friend.

- Questions are a search for playmates.

9

Indigenous Circle Programs

BEFORE DISCUSSING SPECIFIC INDIGENOUS Circle programs, it is important to set the stage by mentioning two metaphors that are in common use in South Pacific cultures, and by then defining pluralistic justice systems that operate in many countries.

Tangles and Disentangling

In some South Pacific cultures, conflicts between individuals or between groups are referred to as "tangles," and the term "disentangling" is used to refer to cultural activities in which people attempt to straighten out their tangled relationships. Picture a snarl of barbed wire that would present a daunting challenge to anyone charged with straightening it. The disentangling metaphor[1] refers to a process rather than an endpoint, and brings sharp focus to the importance of clear communication patterns and good relationships—both key opportunities inherent in Circle processes.

Pluralistic Justice Systems

In many cultures, a two-tiered system of justice exists. When disputes cannot be disentangled in Talking Circles within the community, they are taken to a state formal legal system—whether the community comprises citizens in a Turkish village, fishermen on an isolated island off the Atlantic coast, or sheep and goat herders in Sardinia.

As Laura Nader and Harry S. Todd Jr. emphasize:

> Those who believe that order cannot be achieved without law in the Western sense will find that clearly this is not so. . . . Those who

1. White and Watson-Gegeo, "Disentangling Discourse," 3.

believe that Western law best provides for equality before the law should watch the operation of law in a village court.[2]

> Sardinia provides an excellent example of a particular form of legal pluralism, in which two strong and thriving legal systems operate within the same society—that of the Italian state, and that of the Sard shepherd—but in which the legitimacy of the latter is not recognized by the state. . . . In many areas of conflict Sards do indeed employ the mechanisms of the state legal system. In one crucial and important area, however—in disputes relating to animal theft—Sard shepherds almost universally prefer to avoid the state legal system in favor of their own.[3]

As documented by Sard shepherds, the Circle process can be a meaningful component of pluralistic justice systems. It gives citizens a way to disentangle many issues *within* their own communities, with reliance on a police force and a formal legal system to address issues of safety, and to act as a backup when face-to-face meetings are not successful.

Let's now direct our attention to justice systems that have operated successfully for thousands of years within indigenous communities—from which we can learn a great deal as we endeavor to improve the way in which we interact with each other in the United States.

Six indigenous-culture-based Circle programs that have been well documented in the literature are: (1) Peacemaking Circles (Canada),[4] (2) the Navajo Peacemaker Court (Arizona),[5, 6] (3) Family Group Conferencing (New Zealand),[7] (4) *ho'oponopono* (Hawai'i),[8, 9] (5) *pancayat* (Fiji),[10] and (6) *fono* (Samoa).[11] These programs will be introduced below. Reentry &

---

2. Nader and Todd, "Introduction," 40.

3. Ruffini, "Disputing over Livestock in Sardinia," 223.

4. Pranis et al., *Peacemaking Circles.*

5. Zion, "Dynamics of Navajo Peacemaking."

6. Yazzie, Traditional Navajo Dispute Resolution.

7. McRae and Zehr, *Little Book of Family Group Conferences.*

8. Boggs and Chun, "Ho'oponopono."

9. Pukui et al., *Nānā I Ke Kumu.*

10. Brenneis, "Dramatic Gestures."

11. Duranti, "Doing Things with Words."

Transition Planning Circles[12] and Pono Kaulike,[13] both recently developed restorative justice Circle programs in Hawai'i, will also be described.

It is important to understand that informal Circles are convened every day in every culture in the world, and that no Circle process is necessarily better or worse than any other—with each of them being designed to meet the needs of a particular culture and its citizens. For example, men gather daily in the gastzimmer of the public house in Gottfrieding, Bavaria to discuss and resolve conflicts and to reinforce their sense of community.[14] Women in Gottfrieding also meet daily at "information centers," which are simply the homes of information brokers—women who act as a central clearing house to receive and pass on information. Participation in groups and rules of information exchange for the men and women in Gottfrieding are clearly defined, and the two forums are always gender segregated. In every community in the United States, men meet regularly over coffee to discuss topics such as recent hunting triumphs, business, sports, books, and politics; and women meet regularly to discuss families, politics, books, and philanthropic projects, and to knit or sew together.

Peacemaking Circles (Canada)

Peacemaking Circles evolved from the practice of Sentencing Circles instituted by Judge Barry Stuart in the Yukon.[15, 16] Sentencing Circles allowed justice to be practiced by tribal members themselves in many cases of wrongdoing; they became an opening for use of the Circle process in many other aspects of the Canadian justice system. Peacemaking Circles build on four premises: (1) every human being wants to be connected to others in a good way; (2) everybody shares core values that indicate what connecting in a good way means; (3) being connected in a good way and acting from our values are not always easy to do; and, (4) given a safe place, we can discover our core values and uncover our desire to be positively connected. Peacemaking Circles invite a shift from punishment to healing, from individual efforts to group accountability, from dependence on the state for the

12. Walker and Greening, *Reentry & Transition Planning Circles.*

13. Walker and Hyashi, "Pono Kaulike."

14. Todd, "Litiginous Marginals."

15. Stuart, *Building Community Justice Partnerships.*

16. Pranis et al., *Peacemaking Circles.*

resolution of problems to greater reliance on communities, and on justice as a path to "getting well" instead of "getting even."

Peacemaking Circles are inclusive, and are a safe environment that encourages people to speak from their hearts without fear of judgment or retribution. Peacemaking Circles bring people together, help them bond into communities, and help them develop trust and the willingness to work diligently to resolve issues together—regardless of their difficulty. In the words of Judge Stuart:

> Peacemaking Circles are not just about justice. (Peacemaking Circles are as much about community development as they are about justice.) . . . Peacemaking Circles are not short-term solutions, but rather are investments in the community's future. *The principal value of Community Peacemaking Circles cannot be measured by what happens to offenders, but rather by what happens to communities.*[17]

Peacemaking Circles hold firmly to ten values: (1) respect, (2) honesty, (3) trust, (4) humility, (5) sharing, (6) inclusivity, (7) empathy, (8) courage, (9) forgiveness, and (10) love. Strategies that are recognizable in our Western formal legal system include judgment, accusation, deception, manipulation, insensitivity, arrogance, aggressiveness, and grudge holding—all of which force people apart and make them feel unsafe. The difference between the formal legal system in the United States and Peacemaking Circles is profound.

A clear statement of the power of Peacemaking Circles, and of the difference between them and the Canadian formal legal system, comes from Judge Stuart, who was a representative of the Crown for many years. During his time on the bench, he struggled with the inability of the courts to address the emotional needs of everyone affected by crime, including court professionals:

> As a judge, I listened to the suffering, isolation, and injustices that both led people to commit crimes and that their crimes caused in the lives of others. I understood and then accepted that the need to be impartial required that neither I nor other professionals show the pain and anger we felt. So I did not shout with rage or release the tears welling up from deep within me. While my emotional restraint honored court practices, it dishonored the stories of the people whose lives marched through the court—a march that

17. Stuart, *Building Community Justice Partnerships*, 109.

allowed neither their wounded spirits nor their painful emotions to be addressed.

Like many judges and other professionals in the court process, our restraint comes at a price—a price we realize long after our families and friends recognize it. Our restraint either hardens our hearts or rips into our capacity to joyously embrace life, or both. I screamed in rage on wilderness walks and broke into tears at nothing at all or at seemingly innocuous events. When deep emotions are shut down, they do not disappear. They emerge in other forms in many parts of our lives. I believed there had to be a more respectful, more holistic way to embrace all the aspects of crime—aspects that the court shuts out.[18]

The work of Judge Stuart is also documented in the video *Circle Sentencing: A Yukon Justice Experiment*—to which I credit the beginning of my personal restorative justice journey—and in the video *Circles. It's About Justice. It's About Healing.*

The Peacemaking Circle premises of connectedness, inclusivity, sharing core values, acting from those values, trust, and providing a safe place are the same premises that have guided Community Circles since its inception.

Navajo Peacemaker Court (Arizona)

James Zion and Robert Yazzie explain the legal and spiritual tenets of the Navajo justice system, and the differences between it and the formal legal system in the United States:

> Peacemaking is an indigenous Native American form of dispute resolution and a leading example of restorative justice. Restorative justice, unlike adjudication and the prevailing patterns of world criminal justice systems, views crime and offending as a conflict between individuals that results in injuries to victims, with a process that seeks to reconcile parties and repair the injury caused by a dispute though the active participation of victims, offenders, and communities to find solutions to conflict.[19]

Navajo law comes from relationships—from the most immediate to everyone and everything. Navajos believe that every person is a judge. A

18. Pranis et al., *Peacemaking Circles*, 71–72.
19. Zion, "Dynamics of Navajo Peacemaking," 1.

judge is someone who sees a situation and applies values—shared feelings about the way to do things—to tell people what to do about it. Navajo law puts everyone on the same level, in a Circle of equality, for equality in decision, outcome, and sharing.

> Adjudication uses authority, rank and power, but that does not necessarily work. I can try to make someone else obey the rules using force. I can make a threat to punish, but what happens when I go away? When I turn my back, that person will usually return to what he was doing in the first place. What if I deal with that person in a different way? Instead of threatening to punish, I deal with that person as an equal. Also, I bring in others to address the problem. We all talk about what it is and have an opinion about it. We speak with the wrongdoer, give our opinions, and ask him to respond back. We use our relationship with him to come to agreements. Then, when I walk away, everyone knows what was said; everyone agrees on an outcome. I can turn my back, because everyone who was there knows the agreement and is there to enforce it. It's not a matter of threats—it's an agreement everyone knows and follows.[20]

Navajos view justice as a complete view of life and not as a legal process where an individual wins or loses. Navajos view their justice method as a ceremony, and begin it with prayer that summons supernatural beings to take part in the process.

The second phase is "talking things out," where everyone expresses their feelings. An offender has the opportunity to listen to the charges and the impact of their conduct on the person complaining. When the accused offender has had the opportunity to hear those things and the feelings associated with them, then he or she has an opportunity to respond. "Talking things out" leads to verification of who did what to whom and why.

The third phase involves a form of teaching by the peacemaker, who knows the traditional Navajo values, and expresses them by relating what happened in creation times to the problem at hand. He can point to similar disputes or problems in the past, relate who went through them, and show how the situation was resolved. This is the phase in which people move from "head thinking" to "heart thinking"—to have empathy for others.

The fourth phase is discussion of the barriers to finding a solution. Such barriers might include denial ("I don't have a drinking problem"), minimization ("It's part of our tradition to have sex with a foster child"),

20. Yazzi, "Traditional Navajo Dispute Reolution," 7–8.

or externalization ("It's the system that's to blame"). Peacemaking deals with excuses nicely. In the Navajo Peacemaker Court, a DWI defendant doesn't tell his story to the judge; he tells it to his family. He tells it to his spouse, to his mother, to his brothers and sisters, and to those who know him best. They know what is really going on, they set him straight. Relatives are present to separate truth from fiction and to stop the excuses. They are also there to assist victims and protect them from being abused again. Discussion by everyone involved separates truth from fiction and reality from unreality.

The fifth phase is consensus. A full discussion of problems, in light of reality, produces a good plan. The final decision works because we reconcile people in continuing relationships using respect.

The sixth phase is reconciliation. One of our judges described the "winner takes all" system of justice as one party going out of the courtroom with his tail in the air, and the other going out with his tail between his legs. If, instead, you use methods that promote reconciliation, you will resolve the conflicts that underlie ongoing problems. A judgment in a "win-lose" system tells people what they must do. An agreement in peacemaking commits parties to what they will do. An agreement is better than a judgment.

The seventh and final phase of peacemaking is closure with a prayer.

> In Anglo dispute resolution, only those who are immediately involved in the dispute participate. In a courtroom that is the plaintiff and the defendant. In alternative dispute resolution, it is only the people who are directly connected with the dispute. For example, in a divorce case, it is only the husband and wife. Aren't other people affected by divorce? What about the children? What about the couple's parents? What about neighbors? What about co-workers? Marital discord affects them too.
>
> Think of a legal conflict as a "zone of dispute." In Anglo law, only the husband and wife are within the zone when there is conflict between them. In Navajo law, the couple's children, parents, and others are a part of the problem—or are affected by it—so they are also within the zone of dispute. They are there, because they are a part of it. They all have opinions which come from their values, so they are all judges in the process.[21]

Navajo peacemakers are community leaders whose leadership depends on respect and persuasion, not on a position of power and authority. The immediate disputants are not the only participants; they include

21. Ibid., 8–9.

relatives as well, including persons related by clan affiliation as well as by blood. They participate in the process and have significant input in the form of expressing opinions about the facts and the effects of the dispute, the parties' conformity to Navajo values, and the proper outcome of the dispute. Navajo values are the foundation of law, and the "talking things out" process permits the group to decide what the applicable law happens to be. There are no discussions of rules or "principles of law" to be applied to a dispute; instead there is an interactive discussion of the problem and what the group feels about how it should be resolved. The goal of Navajo peacemaking is reconciliation of the parties in dispute, and the process results in the participants co-creating a new shared reality or perception about the conflict and each other that allows them to move forward in their lives. The healing and reconciliation goals of the Navajo Peacemaker Court are the same as those encompassed by the Community Circles program.

Family Group Conferencing (New Zealand)

The focus of Family Group Conferencing (FGC) is on the restoration of re-lationships.[22] In New Zealand, FGC grew from a pressing need. Thousands of children—especially members of minority groups—were being removed from their homes and placed in foster care or institutions. The juvenile jus-tice system was overburdened and ineffective. Maori leaders pointed out that the Western system of justice was a foreign imposition. In the Maori cultural tradition, judges did not mete out punishment. Instead, the whole community was involved, and the intended outcome was repair. Instead of focusing on blame, they wanted to know why, because they argued that finding the cause of crime is part of resolving it. Instead of punishment ("Let shame be the punishment" is a Maori proverb), they were concerned with healing and problem-solving. Because of these concerns, in the late 1980s the New Zealand government initiated a process of listening to com-munities throughout the country. Through this listening process, the Maori recommended that the resources of the extended family and the commu-nity be the source of any effort to address these issues. FGC emerged as the central tool for doing this. New Zealand's legal system thereby became the first in the world to institutionalize a form of restorative justice, and FGC became the hub of New Zealand's entire juvenile justice system.

22. McRae and Zehr, *Little Book of Family Group Conferences*.

While there is often a common overall pattern to FGCs, each one is adapted to the presented situation. Organized and led by a Youth Justice Coordinator, FGCs are designed to support offenders as they take responsibility for and change their behavior, empower the offenders' families to play an important role in the process, and address the victims' needs. Unlike restorative justice systems elsewhere, this group formulates the *entire* outcome of the case—not just restitution. Importantly, they do so by consensus. In New Zealand, FGCs are the norm and the courtroom is the backup.

The seven primary goals of youth justice in New Zealand are: (1) diversion, (2) accountability, (3) involving the victim, (4) involving and strengthening the offender's family, (5) consensus decision-making, (6) cultural appropriateness, and (7) due process. The seven guiding principles of youth justice are: (1) criminal proceedings should be avoided unless the public interest requires otherwise; (2) criminal justice processes should not be used to provide assistance such as protection, residence, or care; (3) families should be strengthened; (4) children should be kept in the community if at all possible; (5) the child or young person's age must be taken into account; (6) personal development should be promoted using the least restrictive option; and (7) the interests of the victim must be considered.

In Western legal processes—in which the offender is held accountable only to the state—the offender has very little connection to the offense, the victim, the family, or the community where the offense occurred. Any punitive consequence for the offense is viewed as an act of vengeance by the community, and further contributes to offender isolation. This does not help the offender understand the real impact of what he or she has done.

> Within a three-year period, Wellington experienced about a two-thirds drop in youth offending. In 1996, we addressed 554 charges. In 1999, we addressed 174. The number of Conferences required dropped over the same period from 160 to 78. We believe it was due to three main factors: effective Family Group Conferences, close working between the police and the Youth Justice Coordinator, and a collaborative, community-based initiative to address the causes of offending behavior.[23]

The restorative principles espoused by and applied in Family Group Conferencing in New Zealand are the same ones that are inherent in the design of the Community Circles program, and the observed accountability and healing results are equally as meaningful.

23. Ibid., 62.

Ho'oponopono (Hawai'i)

Boggs and Chun[24] and Pukui, Haerteg, and Lee[25] have contributed to the following statement of the principles of *ho'oponopono*. Ho'oponopono is a restorative justice process that means to set things right, to correct, to restore and maintain good relationships among family and between family and supernatural powers. Ho'oponopono is the specific family conference in which relationships are "set right" through prayer, discussion, confession, repentance, and mutual restitution and forgiveness. Ho'oponopono is getting the family together to find out what is wrong—maybe to find out why someone is sick, or the cause of a family quarrel—then, with discussion and repentance and restitution and forgiveness, and always with prayer, to set right what was wrong. In ho'oponopono, people talk openly about their feelings—as a safety valve, as one step toward handling old quarrels or grudges, and even more importantly as prevention so that minor disputes will not grow into big grievances.

An elder, a "head," or a recognized healer—a senior person who has tact, sensitivity, verbal ability, and an intuitive sense of group dynamics—leads ho'oponopono. It begins with prayer. Then a statement of the problem is made, and the transgression discussed. The leader is the only one who conducts prayer, questions others, reprimands, instructs, and interprets. The only words spoken by other participants are in confession, apology, or request for forgiveness and acceptance of it. Family members are expected to work through problems and to cooperate—to "loosen," "release," and "cut" the entanglement; to not "hold fast to the fault." One or more periods of silence may be taken for reflection on the entanglement of emotions and injuries. Everyone's feelings are acknowledged. Then confession, repentance, and forgiveness take place. Everyone releases each other, letting go. They cut off the past, and together they close the event with a ceremonial feast.

Ho'oponopono, which might continue for days, is a supreme effort at self-help on a responsible, adult level; it has a spiritual dimension vital to the Hawaiian people. When Christianity came to Hawai'i, missionaries and Christianized Hawaiians looked down on ho'oponopono for over a century, and fewer and fewer Hawaiians have continued to practice this supreme effort in self-help. Even though incomplete or distorted explanations and

24. Boggs and Chun, Ho'oponopono.
25. Pukui, Haertig, et al., *Nānā I Ke Kumu.*

practices of hoʻoponopono abound today, its premises continue to be the sum total of prayer, discussion, arbitration, contrition, restitution, forgiveness, and releasing—and the thorough looking into layers of action and feeling. The following principles in the formalized version of hoʻoponopono include: (1) discovering the cause of trouble (2) curing or preventing physical illness, depression, or anxiety; (3) resolving interpersonal problems; and (4) untangling or freeing agents from transgressions against spirits and gods as well as humans. Some form of apology and forgiveness is considered an essential element in all forms of hoʻoponopono.

> *Hoʻoponopono* may well be one of the soundest methods to restore and maintain good family relationships that any society has ever devised.[26]

Restoring and maintaining good relationships, as practiced in Hawaiian culture, is a basic tenet of Community Circles and many other Circle programs.

Pancayat (Fiji)

The summary of the *pancayat* event presented below comes from the work of Brenneis.[27] The pancayat ("council of five") is a public event for the mediation of disputes in Bhatgaon, a Fijian Indian community on the island of Vanua Levu. It is concerned not with emotion but with questions of fact; it is highly decorous, restrained, and subject to very narrow relevance rules. The pancayat is considered by Fijian Indians to be a very powerful occasion for social mending, for repairing damaged interpersonal relations, and for restoring amity. It affects the broader village public as well as those immediately involved; disputants and audience alike must be satisfied. A practical resolution alone is insufficient. As one man declared during a pancayat:

> The political work is finished; religious work is remaining.[28]

Pancayat sessions are planned and convened by a committee comprising elected officers of the disputants' religious association. Pancayats involve direct talk about specific events and personalities. Allegations that in most contexts would lead to revenge are discussed at length and without

26. Ibid., 70.
27. Brenneis, "Dramatic Gestures."
28. Ibid., 219.

repercussions. While they are concerned that factual evidence will be presented, the conveners also want to manage the presentation of evidence in such a way that neither party will be completely vanquished. Reinstating the good reputations of both disputants is a central goal. Discourse in the pancayat takes the form of testimony under oath, and various deities comprise an important secondary audience, insuring the truthfulness of eyewitness accounts. Through testimony, an official and definitive account of events crucial to the development of a dispute is publicly constructed. It becomes the basis for later discussion, and for a new baseline against which the subsequent behavior of the disputants can be measured. Members of the committee interview a series of witnesses, each of whom has sworn to give truthful testimony. In contrast to courtrooms in the United States, there is no adversarial questioning. Only the committee can ask questions, and questions compel answers. The committee has a clear prospective interest in future relationships between the disputants, and an emotionally constrained and retrospective focus is the most effective way of insuring a successful outcome.

After the last witness, there is no summing up, no discussion, and no decision by the committee. The disputants are not embarrassed by any directly suggested solution, and the committee members do not overstep their roles. Testimony establishes a single and noncontradictory account of crucial events. These publicly acknowledged facts are seen to stand on their own merit. The pancayat allows the public restoration of good names.

Although many of the Fijian Indian religious and cultural mores are foreign to the dominant culture in the United States, it is of interest to note that many of the tenets of the pancayat process are similar to the principles and practices of all restorative justice programs, including Community Circles. Community involvement, healing, no designation of winners or losers, restoration of good names and relationships, and the welcoming of miscreants or combatants back into the community are all components of the pancayat process. Retribution by word or act is considered anathema to the future well-being of the community, and has no part in the process. Differences between the procedures and outcomes of the pancayat process and those of the formal legal system in the United States are clear.

Fono (Samoa)

A *fono* is a western Samoan social event. As Alessandro Duranti has documented,[29] Samoans are very rank conscious; titled people (*matai*) have the right and duty to sit in a village fono, while untitled people (*taulele'a*) do not. Conflict management in a fono is a cooperative endeavor that provides for public understanding, and creates the context for change. Fonos take place irregularly, depending on the needs of community leaders to avoid or solve a crisis. A kava ceremony opens the fono—kava being a drink made by steeping the shredded root of the kava (*yagona*) plant in water. Having participated in kava ceremonies in Fiji, I attest to the circular format in which the ceremony is conducted, and to its sacred significance for the participants.

The opening orator's speech first recognizes the work of those who provided the kava, then makes a "thanksgiving to God." The orator's speech goes on to refer to one or more important events in Samoan history through the metaphor of "mornings of the past," after which the orator acknowledges the dignity or sanctity of the chiefs, and issues a formal greeting and praise to all the important titles of the village, one by one. The agenda is then announced, with the orator ending his speech by metaphorically referring to the wish for "clear skies," that is, for good health for the participants. Samoans have several expressions that characterize their view of a fono: "make beautiful, decorate"; "make the village beautiful, settle the conflicts within the village"; and "take care of a relationship." The convocation of a fono is the attempt to make life orderly and more predictable, to "cut the weeds," remove the bad feelings, and make the village beautiful again.

Following the ceremonial opening speech, the points of agreement among participants are stressed, such as their willingness to get together and arrive at a decision that would satisfy both the chiefs and the participants. Only after the shared goals and background have been stressed do speakers get into the details of the crisis. During the discussion part of the fono, each speaker tends to embed the more controversial or accusatory statements within outer layers of assertions about harmony, shared understanding, and wishful thinking.

It is in the process of accusing, shaming, blaming, as well as discussing possible solutions to a particular conflict that Samoans create a context for understanding more than what is being explicitly discussed. An apology to

---

29. Duranti, "Doing Things with Words."

the assembly, or at least to some of its members, is an important outcome of any fono that discusses direct or potential breaches of social norms. One might think of the entire fono process of disentangling as a series of moves toward reconciliation, with apology being one of the last steps.

The focus in the fono process on an opening sacred ceremony, on the connectedness of all participants, on giving thanks for the opportunity to participate, on restoration of good relationships, and on the goal of reestablishing harmony in the community are all goals that are at the heart of the Community Circles program.

Reentry and Transition Planning Circles (Hawai'i)

In Hawai'i, over 60 percent of people released from state prisons without supervision (probation or parole) reoffend—on average, within twelve months of their release. Lorenn Walker and Rebecca Greening emphasize the importance of helping people in their transition back into their communities:

> Reentry is the process of leaving prison and returning to society. Reentry is not a form of supervision, like parole. Reentry is not a goal, like rehabilitation or reintegration. Reentry is not an option. Reentry reflects the iron law of imprisonment: they all come back."
> . . . Sentencing processes do not ask people pleading guilt to address how their behavior affected others, or ask defendants what they could possibly do to repair the harm they caused. . . .
> Besides overlooking accountability, our criminal justice system also largely ignores the needs of those hurt by crime, who are often the perpetrator's loved ones.[30]

In Hawai'i, Reentry and Transition Planning Circles give incarcerated people and their loved ones an opportunity to address their need to heal and rebuild their lives, beginning with reconciliation. This Circle process can be a time when incarcerated people accept accountability for their actions, and build a future story of who they want to be and how they want to live when they are released. The Reentry and Transition Planning program is built on a competency-based, solution-focused model that minimizes emphasis on past failings and problems, and instead focuses on clients' strengths, previous successes, and potential.

30. Walker and Greening, *Reentry & Transition Planning Circles*, 21.

In Hawai'i, the Circle process is called Huikahi Restorative Circles. In Hawaiian, *hui* means "group" and *kahi* means "individual," and for purposes of the Reentry and Transition Planning process, the two come together to mean a mutual understanding or covenant.

Huikahi Circles are made available to prisoners early in their period of incarceration, with the people who participate in the Circle being selected entirely from a list provided by the incarcerated individual.

> An imprisoned person voluntarily invites her loved ones, along with a prison representative, to meet in a facilitated Circle provided by a community organization. . . . The purpose of the Circle is twofold. First, the Circle process assists the incarcerated person in preparing a detailed written plan that addresses his/her needs, including reconciliation and assists them in establishing a support system for a successful return to the community. Second, the Circle provides an opportunity for loved ones to address ways that the incarcerated person may work to repair any harm they have caused to others.[31]

The Reentry and Transition Planning Circle process views incarcerated people as having the capacity to manage their lives, and as having the ability to address the harm that their behavior and incarceration have caused to others and to themselves. The Circle process is a chance for incarcerated people to learn how to create positive futures by letting them figure out what they want, how they may get what they want, and how to manage their lives.

The Huikahi Circle program has six steps: (1) introduction of the program at prisons, (2) an application process, (3) a solution-focused interview of Circle applicants, (4) convening the Circle, (5) conducting the Circle, and (6) preparing and distributing the transition plan document.

All 340 Huikahi Circle participants through 2011 (including prisoners and their supporters) have reported that the Circle in which they participated was a positive experience. The 30 percent recidivism rate for those who have participated in Huikahi Circles is significantly lower than Hawai'i's overall 54.7 percent recidivism rate for formerly incarcerated people.

> Correction programs and prisons need to work for rehabilitation, and not dehumanizing and further criminalizing people. . . .
> These reentry and transition planning Circles help people deal

31. Ibid., 9.

with guilt, shame, and other painful emotions when a loved one is imprisoned. The Circles also help incarcerated people see that they have support who can help them "paddle their canoes." The Circles engage all, and shine more light into lives of all participants, including prison staff. Circles can help rehabilitate incarcerated people, heal families, and transform prison cultures.[32]

The reentry work that we have done in Community Circles to help adult felons reintegrate into the Missoula community equates well with the goals and accomplishments of the program instituted in Hawai'i by Walker and Greening.

Pono Kaulike (Hawai'i)

Lorenn Walker and Hon. Leslie Hayashi have worked closely with the Pono Kaulike program.[33] Pono Kaulike—meaning equal rights and justice for all—is a pilot program for people in Hawai'i who plead guilty to criminal offenses, for the people hurt by the crimes, and for their supporters. By giving people a voice, and the opportunity to consider what they and others need to deal with the consequences of crime, they are given the opportunity to learn and to improve their lives. Because the principles of Pono Kaulike parallel the principles of Community Circles so closely, a description of the results of this program merit inclusion in this chapter.

In 2000, Chief Justice Ronald T. Y. Moon (Honolulu) issued the "Judiciary's Resolution Concerning Restorative Justice and the Concept of *Pono Kaulike*." The resolution signified a dedication to deliver services and resolve disputes in a balanced manner that provides attention to all the participants in the justice system, including parties, attorneys, witnesses, jurors, and other community members. Pono Kaulike gives people an opportunity to address underlying emotional and personal issues that need to be talked about—especially when family, fellow employees, neighbors, or those with an intimate relationship have a future together. Three types of restorative practices have evolved:[34] (1) A Restorative Conference occurs when the defendant, victim, and supporters of both parties meet in a group; the parties then enter into a written Restorative Conference Agreement. (2) A Restorative Dialogue occurs when the defendant and victim meet

32. Ibid., 74.

33. Walker and Hayashi, "Pono Kaulike."

34. Ibid., 10.

without family or friends; the parties then enter into a Restorative Dialogue Agreement. And (3) a Restorative Session occurs when the parties are unwilling to meet with each other, but wish to meet with a facilitator. The session may result in a Restorative Plan Agreement.

A total of sixty-one Pono Kaulike participants were surveyed for their satisfaction with the process immediately following their participation. Fifty-nine participants reported that the process was positive, with two reporting that it was mixed—but finding other aspects positive. Only one person reported any aspect of a Pono Kaulike intervention as negative. Although recidivism is only one measure of restorative justice programs, the results from Hawai'i are encouraging. Of twenty-one people in a control group not afforded Pono Kaulike services, the recidivism rate was 57 percent. Of the thirty-eight people in the experimental group—those who received Pono Kaulike intervention—the recidivism rate was 29 percent. The significance of these results is naturally tempered by the small sample sizes, and ongoing evaluation is in progress. A conclusion of the work conducted, as of 2009, is that:

> Without rehabilitating people and assisting victims cope with the effects of wrongdoing, we put our communities at risk for increased conflict and crime.[35]

35. Ibid., 7.

10
Learning from the Past
Our Guide for Designing the Future

Those who cannot remember the past are condemned to repeat it.[1]

BECAUSE I AM POSITING the use of the Circle process as a means for achieving better interactions among human beings today, it's important to lock in the wisdom that has worked so well for thousands of years. Let's do that now, by summarizing the salient features of the above Circle programs.

Peacemaking Circles invite a shift from punishment to healing, from individual efforts to group accountability, from dependence on the state to greater reliance on communities, and to justice as a path to "getting well" instead of "getting even." Peacemaking Circles help people develop trust and the willingness to work together to resolve issues, regardless of their difficulty. They are inclusive, and are a safe environment that encourages people to speak from their hearts without fear of judgment or retribution. Peacemaking Circles are a springboard for coming together in ways that are open, spontaneous, freeing, and unlimited in possibilities. People feel listened to and valued. Peacemaking Circles hold firmly to ten values: (1) respect, (2) honesty, (3) trust, (4) humility, (5) sharing, (6) inclusivity, (7) empathy, (8) courage, (9) forgiveness, and (10) love.

The Navajo Peacemaker Court views justice as a ceremony that begins and ends with a prayer. "Talking things out" is the path to determining who did what to whom and why. Participants are not only the immediate disputants, but their relatives as well. They participate in the process and have significant input in the form of expressing opinions about both the facts and the effects of the dispute, the parties' conformity to Navajo values, and the proper outcome of the dispute. A full discussion of problems produces a good plan. There are no discussions of rules or "principles of law" to be

1. Santanaya, *Life of Reason*, vol. 1, 244.

applied to a dispute; rather, the process involves an interactive discussion of the problem and what the group feels about how it should be resolved. In the Navajo Peacemaker Court, a DWI defendant, for instance, doesn't tell his story to the judge; he tells it to his family members who know him best. Relatives are present to separate truth from fiction and to stop the excuses. They are also there to assist victims and protect them from being abused again. The goal of Navajo peacemaking is reconciliation, and results in participants co-creating a new shared reality or perception about the conflict and each other, that allows them to move forward in their lives. A judgment in a "win-lose" system tells people what they must do. An agreement in the Navajo Peacemaker Court commits parties to what they will do. An agreement is better than a judgment.

Family Group Conferencing involves the whole community, and focuses on restoring relationships. Family Group Conferencing works to understand the causes of crime as a way of preventing it, addresses victims' needs, supports offenders, and empowers families. Youths should not be involved in criminal proceedings unless the public interest requires otherwise. Families should be strengthened. Children should be kept in the community if at all possible. Personal development should be promoted using the least restrictive option, and the interests of the victim must be considered. Punitive consequences for offenses are viewed by the community as acts of vengeance, which further contribute to an offender's isolation.

Ho'oponopono means to make things right, to correct, to restore and maintain good relationships. In many Pacific societies, including Hawai'i, the metaphor for conflict is "getting tangled," and making things right is "disentangling." Ho'oponopono gets the family together to find out what is wrong. Then, with discussion, acknowledgment of feelings, repentance, restitution, and forgiveness, the group sets right what was wrong.

The Fijian pancayat focuses on repairing damaged relations. It involves the whole village and manages the presentation of evidence in such a way that neither party is completely vanquished. Reinstating the good reputations of both disputants is a central goal. Through testimony before a committee of respected individuals, an official and definitive account of events is publicly constructed. In contrast to United States courtrooms, there is no adversarial questioning. After the last witness, there is no summing up, and the committee makes no decision. The disputants are not embarrassed by any directly suggested solution. The publicly acknowledged facts stand on their own merit. The pancayat allows for the public restoration of good names.

The Samoan fono is opened with a sacred ceremony. Through a process of accusing, shaming, and blaming as well as discussing possible solutions to a particular conflict, participants create a context for understanding more than what is being explicitly discussed. Speakers embed controversial or accusatory statements within layers of assertions about harmony, shared understanding, and wishful thinking. The fono process of disentangling is a series of moves toward reconciliation—with apology being one of the last steps.

Reentry and Transition Planning Circles help people deal with guilt, shame, and other painful emotions when a loved one is imprisoned. The Circles also help incarcerated people see that they have support that can help them when they are released. Reentry and Transition Planning Circles treat incarcerated people as having strengths, potential, and the capacity to manage their lives. Incarcerated people prepare a detailed written plan that addresses their needs when they are released from prison, including reconciliation, and the plan then assists them in establishing a support system for a successful return to the community. Reentry and Transition Planning Circles can help rehabilitate incarcerated people, heal families, and transform prison cultures.

Pono Kaulike gives people an opportunity to address underlying emotional and personal issues that need to be talked about. Without rehabilitating people and assisting victims to cope with the effects of wrongdoing, our communities are at risk for increased conflict and crime. Pono Kaulike is dedicated to delivering services and resolving disputes in a balanced manner that provides attention to all the participants in the justice system—including parties, attorneys, witnesses, jurors, and other community members. By focusing on what people need to deal with the consequences of crime, they are given the opportunity to learn and to improve their lives.

The wisdom from these deep cultural traditions will be woven into the following applications of the Circle process.

11

Applications of the Circle Process in Our Lives

The Tie Between Restorative Justice and the Circle Process

RESTORATIVE JUSTICE IS THE premise within which the Circle process operates. The healing principle is most commonly viewed in the context of the needs of victims, accountability for offenders, and the needs of the community. The same principle of healing applies as well to Circles within families, neighborhoods, and community interest organizations, between teachers and parents, between students, and within and between business organizations. The principle includes a provision for a safe meeting place in which opinions, concerns, and ideas can be voiced without interruption or judgment—a good space for "talking things out." The principle includes the responsibility to build on the good points of others and to not criticize speakers for the purpose of self-aggrandizement.

The Circle process is restorative in that it includes the principles of making things right, disentangling, encouraging discussion by affected parties, giving equal voice to *all* participants, and relying on the wisdom of *all* participants in decision-making. Participants share thoughts and ideas openly, with a focus on hope and possibilities. Participants feel listened to and valued. Relationships are buoyed.

Circles address underlying emotional and personal issues that need to be talked about. They treat individuals who have been harmed, and those who have caused harm, as having strengths, potential, and the capacity to manage their lives in a good way. The Circle process allows for discussion of the issues that underlie inappropriate actions, without mention of sanctions or punishment. Agreements reached in Circles commit parties to what they will do, rather than what they must do. The Circle process, by providing a safe time and space in which people can tell their stories, is a key component in fulfilling the needs of victims, offenders, and communities.

Restorative justice focuses on repairing inequities of the past. Circles also have an important role to play in forward-focused design projects. Circles provide a safe, respectful venue in which people can float creative ideas without fear of criticism, and in which participants feel comfortable building on ideas brought forward by others. Restorative justice is an overarching set of values. The Circle process is a way to make restorative justice come to life.

We'll now look at the principles of restorative justice and the Circle process in the following contexts: the formal legal system, families, neighborhoods, schools, the workplace, and civic group processes. Some overlap of the ideas presented will occur, and that's fine. The Circle process has universal applications, and overlapping is done by design.

Crime and the Formal Legal System

> Restorative justice is a process to involve, to the extent possible, those who have a stake in a specific offense and to collectively identify and address harms, needs, and obligations, in order to heal and put things as right as possible.[1]

The emphasis of restorative justice is on rebuilding relationships, and on integrating wrongdoers back into the community with an opportunity to be productive members—rather than on isolating them and giving them cause for spite. The restorative Circle process is a powerful way in which to help all factions impacted by crime move to a better path.

Reduced recidivism may be a byproduct of restorative justice, but it is employed first of all because it is the right thing to do. Victims' rights should be addressed, offenders should be encouraged to take responsibility, and those affected by an offense should be involved in the process—regardless of whether or not offenders learn from their mistakes and reduce their offending.

If restorative justice were to be taken seriously, our reliance on prisons would be reduced, and the nature of prisons would change significantly. Restorative justice is not necessarily the opposite of retribution, and its approaches can be used in conjunction with and parallel to prison sentences.

1. Zehr, *Little Book of Restorative Justice*, 37.

A primary goal of both retributive justice and restorative justice is for vindication, or to even the score. Both types of justice acknowledge a basic moral intuition that a balance has been thrown off by a wrongdoing. Consequently, the victim deserves something and the offender owes something. Both approaches argue that there must be a proportional relationship between the act and the response. Retributive theory believes that pain will vindicate, but in practice that is often counterproductive for both the victim and the offender. Restorative justice, on the other hand, advances that what truly vindicates is acknowledgement of victims' needs, combined with an active effort to encourage offenders to take responsibility, make right the wrongs, and address the causes of their behavior. By addressing this need to even the score in a positive way, restorative justice has the potential to affirm the value of both victims and offenders, and to help them transform their lives. Restorative justice provides a context in which forgiveness and reconciliation might happen, but this is a choice that is entirely up to the participants.

Zehr suggests the following signposts of restorative justice when harm has been caused:[2]

1. Focus on the harms of crime rather than on the rules that have been broken.

2. Show equal concern and commitment to victims and offenders, involving both in the process of justice.

3. Work toward the restoration of victims, empowering them and responding to their needs as they see them.

4. Support offenders, while encouraging them to understand, accept, and carry out their obligations.

5. Recognize that while obligations may be difficult for offenders, those obligations should not be intended as harms, and they must be achievable.

6. Provide opportunities for dialogue, direct or indirect, between victim and offender as appropriate.

7. Find meaningful ways to involve the community and respond to the community bases of crime.

2. Ibid., 40–41.

8. Encourage collaboration and reintegration of victims and offenders, rather than coercion and isolation.

9. Give attention to the unintended consequences of your actions and program.

10. Show respect to all parties—victims, offenders, justice colleagues.

Because communities are directly impacted by crime, they *must* be considered as stakeholders. Communities must continually engage in dialogue about the conditions that allow crimes and other misdeeds to occur, and they must seize opportunities to rebuild the sense of connectedness that promotes healthy families and neighborhoods.

To firmly cement our understanding of restorative justice, let's look at the terms "victim" and "offender"—labels that are familiar because we hear them every day. In the Community Circles program, we prefer to use the terms "harmed individual" and "wrongdoer," although these *also* distance us from an acknowledgment that we're really talking about people and our fellow human beings. The terms "harmed individual" and "wrongdoer" *do* accurately state what happened *at a point in time*, and they reflect the opportunity, with healing, for victims and offenders to move beyond a criminal act or a community misdeed, and to live more productive and fulfilling lives. Life is dynamic, and labels that can last a lifetime should only be used with careful thought to the implications.

> In short, Circles offer a dramatically different response to crime from the current justice system. By bringing people together to address profound human needs, they help us reach out to each other and discover deeper connections—connections that for some have rarely, if ever, graced their lives.[3]

Whenever crimes or misdeeds have been committed, both those harmed and those who have caused harm have needs. The Circle process affords the opportunity to meet those needs. Let's consider the needs of each of these groups. For simplicity, the terms "victim" and "offender" will be used below.

3. Pranis et al., *Peacemaking Circles*, 29.

Victims' Needs

Restorative justice expands the Circle of stakeholders beyond the government and the person who committed harm, to include victims. Victims need answers to questions about the offense: why it happened and what has happened since. An important element in moving beyond the experience of crime is an opportunity to tell the story of what happened. Often it is important for victims to tell their story to the ones who caused the harm, and to have them understand the impact of their actions. Victims often feel that control has been taken away from them by the offenses they've experienced—control over their property, their bodies, their emotions and their dreams. Involvement in their own cases can be an important way to return a sense of empowerment to them. Monetary restitution by offenders is often important to victims because of actual losses, but symbolic restitution is also important—as recognition of the harm caused.

Victim Circles

Over the past hundred years, the formal legal system has enacted a shift from a balanced focus on victims and offenders to a focus of attention and resources almost exclusively on offenders. The Circle process, designed to treat the needs of both offenders and victims, aspires to correct this imbalance.

The victim's input contributes in numerous ways to the goals of the Circle. Consequently, every effort must be made to encourage and support victims. Victims must feel that their concerns are as pressing and as important as those of the offender. If the victim decides not to participate in the Circle process, assistance and support are still necessary, and a victim's representative should be involved to ensure that the victim's interests are known in the Circle. Preparing for a victim to participate in a Circle should include:

- Deciding if and how a victim will participate;

- Establishing a victim support group;

- Identifying people to participate in the Circle with or on behalf of the victim, and only if the victim wishes them to do so;

- Preparing the victim to ensure that expectations are realistic, to assess needs, and to discuss possible benefits and risks;

- Preparing the victim to speak in the Circle
- Considering restitution possibilities:
  - Work for the victim,
  - Work for the charity of the victim's choice,
  - Restorative community service,
  - Apology,
  - Participation in education or assessment programs,
  - Anything else that feels right and reasonable to all participants.

Pre-Circle preparation offers the best opportunity to protect victims, to facilitate their full involvement, and to ensure that their participation does not jeopardize their safety. Victims must feel sufficiently safe to reveal facts that only they know. Community resources and, in some cases, professional ones must be available to victims throughout the Circle process—to remove fears of repercussions, and to support their participation.

Several years ago, a crime victim approached Community Circles with the following story. A teenager had stolen her vehicle, trashed it, and then driven it into a river. The offender had been apprehended. The harmed person was not wealthy, so monetary compensation for her loss was important. Also of importance was her need to meet with the teenager, face to face, to let him know the impact of his actions on her and, along with him, to agree on a restitution plan that would meet both of their needs. The victim had met with the arresting officer, who was supportive of her plan to speak during the scheduled court hearing. Having the judge's approval for her to speak at the hearing, I met with the victim several times before the court date and helped her practice her words and develop confidence in her message. During the court hearing—attended by the teenager and his mother—the victim was indeed given the opportunity to speak directly to the teenager, although the judge's body language strongly suggested that he was not thrilled with the departure from standard protocol.

As I was standing outside the courtroom with the victim following the hearing, the teenager and his mother emerged; both of them approached the victim, shook her hand, and thanked her for what she had done. When I followed up with the victim a month later, she said that, although the teenager and his mother had moved out of state, restitution was being paid on a regular basis. The simple step of allowing the victim to have voice after having been harmed was a powerful way to put restorative justice into practice.

Offenders' Needs

The formal legal system is concerned with holding offenders accountable, and making sure that they get the punishment they deserve. Little in the process encourages offenders to feel compassion for their victims or to empathize with them. Offenders are not encouraged to face their responsibilities to the people they have harmed, and are given little opportunity to act on those responsibilities—even if they so choose. One of the felons we met with in the Community Circles program was forbidden to have any contact with the person he had harmed. Thus, the parties were never able to address the hurt they each felt; the possibility for forgiveness and/or reconciliation was kept from them. The neutralization strategies—the strategies and rationalizations that offenders often use to distance them from the people they hurt—are never challenged. Unfortunately, then, an offender's sense of alienation from society is heightened by the formal legal process and by the punishment experience.

Offenders need accountability that addresses the harm they have caused, and that encourages responsibility, compassion, and empathy. They need help in understanding the factors that contributed to their offending behavior, encouragement to change their lives, opportunities for treatment for addictions and/or other problems, opportunities for enhancement of personal competencies, and encouragement and support in transitioning back into their communities.

Offender Circles

An offender's charges pending before the court seldom tell even a small fraction of the person's story. By providing offenders a safe place in which to tell their story, the Circle process offers them an opportunity to talk about issues never before discussed, to share feelings that have been buried, and to find clarity about the reasons for events in their life. In one Circle in the Community Circles program, the offender and his two supporters talked about previously unshared family-value issues going back two generations; in another Circle, an offender had a chance to discuss and defuse strong and scary feelings about a second car accident that occurred on the one-year anniversary of a first one.

Whenever Community Circles convenes a Circle for an offender, and a victim is identified (for example, a person from whom wood had been stolen, or a person whose mailbox had been blown up), it is our policy to personally contact the harmed individual, to talk with them about Community Circles, and to offer to convene a Circle for them if they so choose. To date, no victims have requested that a Circle be convened, but all of them have been appreciative of the personal contact and the expression of concern.

The Circle process, as an embodiment of restorative justice, can be brought to bear in positive ways—not only in the formal legal system, but also in many aspects of our personal and communal lives. We will now look at some of these applications.

Family Circles

In family Circles, one or more orientation Circles are first convened to define the issues that need to be discussed. Following this orientation, the Circle format is the same as has been described above.

I sat at a picnic table on the grassy shore of Lake Champlain in Vermont long ago with my mother and my two sisters, and convened a Circle—this before I had even heard the term or knew anything about the Circle process. The issue was whether my mother would enter a retirement facility in New England (where she had spent her entire life), and be near one of her daughters, or move to the dramatically different geographic and cultural setting of Missoula, Montana, and be close to me and my family. Although a talking piece was not used, a respectful conversation was held—with no interruptions—and my mother had a chance to hear from each of her children as she faced the decision that would define her next life chapter. *Her* decision proved to be a good one for her, and her ensuing thirteen years in a retirement community in Missoula, ending at age ninety-nine, were rich and fulfilling. A fond memory of my Mother at age ninety-three is of her dancing at a powwow with Native Americans under the arbor of a Native American dance Circle. As primary caregivers, my wife and I benefitted greatly from my mother's wisdom, and from the numerous visits to Missoula by relatives from across the United States. The Circle process is powerful, whether a Circle is convened formally or informally—with the principle of respectful interaction among participants held high for all to see and abide by.

Another example of a family Circle—this one convened by Community Circles—involved poor communication and bad feelings in a blended family. Two orientation Circles were held, one with the recently married parents, and the other one with just the four teenagers—two from each of the previous families. The parents acknowledged their concern about the poor communication pattern among the teenagers, and voiced their feelings of disconnect with their own, and with the other kids. In their orientation Circle, the four teenagers talked openly with each other and expressed their desire to all become closer. The issue was raised of an upsetting change in bedroom assignments by the parents when the two families blended into one residence. During the ensuing Circle with all six individuals, the bedroom issue was brought forward, and the teenagers for whom it was a significant event had a chance to talk about their feelings. The feelings were acknowledged by the parents and apologizes were offered. In one of the more poignant exchanges that took place, one of the teenagers had the chance to tell her father that she really did not want any more gifts from him, and that all she wanted was his love. *Such a dialogue could never be scripted in the theater!* When the talking piece reached the father, he turned to me and asked if there was a stone in the bowl in the center of the Circle with the word "ouch" on it.

Considering the importance of relationships in indigenous Circle processes, and the opportunity for people to speak openly from their hearts in Circles, and to listen intently, the Circle process was powerful for the above family.

Neighborhood Circles

Neighborhood Circles can be useful for designing enhancement projects, defusing potential crises, managing and resolving contentious issues, and for sharing times of celebration or grief.

Several years ago, a parent approached Community Circles and requested a Circle for her son, four other teenage boys, and their parents. The boys had been apprehended for shoplifting a package of Sudafed. The ensuing Circle comprised fifteen people. During the first passing of the talking piece, each boy admitted to being scared when arrested, and expressed regret for having done something so stupid—lesson learned. On subsequent rounds, the boys talked about some of the pressures they faced daily, both in and out of school, and about the ease of obtaining a banned substance. Some of the parents expressed concern about the substance being a "gateway drug" and about it being illegal, with one parent voicing the opinion, "What's the big deal?" During the Circle, the boys felt safe discussing subjects that had previously been off limits, and the parents felt comfortable voicing their concerns. The Circle was not court mandated and, when asked what they would like to do in the future, every participant voted for holding another Circle because of the good space it provided for talking about important issues.

Nathan, a teenager, got reckless late one night and trashed a mailbox in his neighborhood. Everyone knows Nathan and his family and knows that, although Nathan did a stupid thing, he is not a bad kid. The neighborhood, knowing about the effectiveness of the Circle process, convened a Circle on Nathan's behalf. Nathan, his family members, the elderly couple that was directly affected, and many other neighbors attended. Family members and neighbors spoke about the impact of the event on them, including their fear that such events might be gang related and might mean that they were no longer safe in their homes. Nathan acknowledged his misdeed, and offered to pay for and install a new mailbox. Residents living on either side of the elderly couple suggested that Nathan offer to repair and paint the fence around the elderly couple's home. Nathan gladly agreed to do the work and to pay for the supplies. The Circle closed with neighbors talking about Nathan's positive attributes and offering him their support, and with Nathan expressing thanks for people caring about him.

The above healing scenarios are possible in every neighborhood, and provide a much more positive approach than immediately calling 911. Law enforcement is always available as backup to citizen resolution of community issues.

Neighborhood Circles involve the many complexities of all group processes. For example, it is important to agree on the number of people who will participate; who will sit in the Circle and represent whom; whether an inner Circle and an outer Circle, or other format, will be appropriate if a large number of people wants to participate; what to do when new participants show up unexpectedly; how to handle the media; what guidelines are appropriate; what decision-making process will be used; and what success will look like.

In a neighborhood Circle convened by Community Circles, all of the above factors were present. The contentious issue involved activities of clients using a rescue mission, and the concerns of neighbors living nearby. Petitions had been signed, letters to the editor of the local newspaper had been written, and a few verbal threats had been lobbed. There was concern that, as the weather warmed, tempers would keep pace and violence would erupt. At the request of a neighborhood leader, we assembled a team of four Circle Keepers and met separately with numerous individuals in the neighborhood and with personnel at the rescue mission. These meetings were vital to the later success of the process. Three Circle meetings were held. Introductions—names, personal backgrounds, reasons for attendance, and concerns—were voiced during the rounds of the talking piece in the first Circle. For the first time people saw each other as human beings, with personal stories and names—markedly different from the "us-versus them" labels they had known previously. Individuals on both sides of the issue were able to express their concerns as neighbors, rather than as legal adversaries. The second and third Circle meetings focused in more detail on participants' concerns, and on crafting positive suggestions for future actions—a number of which involved law enforcement, city government, rescue mission leaders, the rail line company whose tracks bordered the mission, and the citizens themselves.

The importance of planning for each Circle meeting cannot be overstated—to consider the flow of the Circle within the allotted time frame, and to consider what might go wrong. In the neighborhood Circles described above, we were able to divide responsibilities between the four Circles Keepers into: (1) planning the meeting room logistics, (2) discussing guidelines, and (3) opening and closing each Circle. These assignments were in addition to each of us sharing from our personal experience banks, as we do in all Circles.

Education Circles

Using the Circle Process in Schools

As stated by Lorraine Stutzman Amstutz and Judy H. Mullet,[4] harnessing the interest and creative energy of students, teachers, and staff members using the Circle process can not only decrease truancy, chronic absentee-

4. Amstutz and Mullet, *Little Book of Restorative Discipline for Schools.*

ism and dropout rates; it can help students develop respect for themselves and others as valued members of the educational community. The Circle process can help students build confidence and, because all participants are equal, compel teachers and staff members to listen closely to students' concerns and ideas. Some suggestions for using the Circle process in schools are as follows:

- Morning Circles:
  - How was your night?
  - What's going on in your life right now?
  - What are your thoughts about today's assignment?
  - Discussing the daily schedule
  - Dealing with behavior problems such as teasing, stealing, fighting
  - Sharing, show-and-tell
  - Goal setting for projects, units, tests, and behavior
  - Evaluating field trips, assemblies, and projects
  - Brainstorming, creative writing, class projects
  - Discussing; news articles, books, and controversial topics
  - Storytelling
  - Student-chosen topics
- End-of-the-day Circles:
  - Sharing something that happened to each person that day
  - Addressing problems that arose during the day
  - Talking about disturbing events in the school or in the outside world
  - Summarizing the events of the day
- Examples of youth-initiated Circles:
  - Working with an adult advisor, a youth group used the Circle process to organize and manage a coffee shop.
  - A group of young people grieving the death of a friend held a Circle to share their grief.

- Two youth facilitated a Circle for younger children in a program for homeless women and children.

- An AmeriCorps youth group working on environmental and health issues in the community met in Circles regularly to work on plans and on issues facing the youth.

- A school chess team used the Circle process to improve focus and support for one another.

- Two youth preparing to leave a correction facility attended a Circle Keeper training in hopes of using the Circle with their friends back in the community.

- Youth from different cultures and speaking different languages met in Circles to learn about one another after tension arose between them on a basketball court.

- A boy who knew about Circles from school asked his mother to hold a Circle with two small cousins who were fighting.

- Youth from several rival gangs in an immigrant community participated in a Circle to explore the possibilities for reducing violence between the gangs.

• Educator, staff, and administration Circles

Two topics that are of concern in schools today are discipline and bullying. Let's look at each of these issues and consider the potential value of the Circle process for dealing with them.

The term "discipline" comes from an Old English word meaning "to teach or train." Discipline is teaching children rules to live by and helping them become socialized into their culture. Discipline can have a short-term goal of stopping inappropriate behavior, and a long-term goal of helping children learn to take responsibility for their own behavior.

Discipline by punishment serves to temporarily restrain a child, but does little to teach self-discipline. The student often questions the nature of the punishment, blaming the punisher rather than taking responsibility for the harm caused by the misbehavior. Punishment continues to be a dominant feature in school discipline because it is quick, easy to administer, and seems to meet the criterion that "at least something was done." Restorative discipline, in contrast to punishment, concerns itself with appropriate consequences that encourage accountability—accountability that emphasizes empathy and repair of harm. Restorative discipline includes the opportunity for creativity to replace strict rules that are more about our need for control or to achieve quick resolution, rather than about our children's lifelong learning. Restorative discipline requires thinking about the behaviors that rules are meant to regulate, more than about the rules themselves.

Restorative discipline (1) acknowledges that relationships are central to building community, (2) builds systems that address misbehavior and harm in a way that strengthens relationships, (3) focuses on the harm done rather than only on rule-breaking; (4) gives voice to the persons harmed, (5) engages in collaborative problem-solving; (6) empowers change and growth, and (7) enhances responsibility.

Because restorative discipline is based on respect and caring, as opposed to adherence to rules, and because all voices—including teachers, staff, administrators, parents, and students—are included in the creative journey to find solutions to problems, the Circle process is ideally suited for advancing and building on the ideas of all participants.

Restorative discipline engages a no-blame framework to support bully-free schools. These "peaceable schools" discourage bullying by creating a caring environment.

> Bullying may be the most common type of violence in schools today. It is reported that almost 30 percent of U.S. teens are either a bully, a target of bullying, or both. Most bullying incidents last less than a minute, with cyber bullying via instant messaging or mass e-mails occurring almost instantaneously. Bullying is defined as a pattern of intentional harm done over time, which can take physical, verbal, or proxemic forms. The last form translates into exclusion through social or personal distance, thus harming relationships.[5]

> Circle processes for educators, staff, and students promote fairness and build supportive relationships necessary for safe schools. Within regularly planned Circles or morning meetings, persons engaged in the education of children become aware of bullying around them, share their experiences of bullying someone and being bullied, learn ways to communicate nonviolently, create guidelines for safe community, and support each other toward healthier ways of thinking and acting.
> When bullying occurs, the goal becomes one of restoration and reintegration for all parties. Restorative community

5. Ibid., 67.

conferences or circles are sometimes held to engage all persons affected by the bullying. This is an occasion for all to hear the harm and to plan steps to accountability and reintegration.[6]

A Community Oriented Policing Services (COPS) report states that a zero-tolerance approach may result in a high level of suspensions, without full comprehension of how behavior needs to and can be changed. It does not solve the problem of the bully, who typically spends more unsupervised time in the home or community if suspended or expelled.

Highlighting some of the key words and phrases in the discipline and bullying sections above is instructive: respect, support, a caring environment, relationships, empathy, accountability, creativity, repair of harm, building community, voice, and collaborative problem-solving. These words and phrases almost seem repetitive, considering their inclusion in all parts of the book so far, and they will continue to appear in our continuing discussion of the restorative Circle process in education.

Experiences in Minnesota Schools

Nancy Riestenberg captures the positive impact of the Circle process in schools in Minnesota:

> Variations on formal processes of restorative justice—victim offender dialogue, family group conferencing, large group conferencing and circles to repair harm, are used in about 40% of Minnesota school districts. Practitioners' report that they modify the processes to fit the needs of the situation, from truancy to possession of banned substances, from bullying to large-scale racial harassment, from morning community circles to restorative goals in education plans. Two years' worth of evaluation in four different school districts shows that restorative practices reduced the number of suspensions and discipline referrals to the office.
>
> In one suburban district, the circle process is ubiquitous. Thirty percent of the staff in the two elementary schools uses circles in their classrooms as a means of community building or problem solving. Ninety-five percent of the teachers call in the restorative justice planner to hold circles to repair harm. The planner goes into every classroom at the beginning of the year, and using the circle process to ensure that everyone is heard, leads the students through a discussion of what they could do each day to

6. Ibid., 68–69.

make the peace in their school. Students are so familiar with the process that a group of students borrowed a talking piece from the planner and held a circle on the playground by themselves.

In one of these elementary schools the circle process helped to reduce the number of daily referrals to the office for violent offenses from 7 to a little less than 2. Also, out-of-school suspensions were cut in half from 30 to 15 between the 1998-1999 and 1999-2000 school years. At the other elementary school in the district, out-of-school suspensions dropped from 27 to 4 over the same two years and out-of-school suspensions at the junior high went from 110 to 65.[7]

A director of an alternative learning center filed the following report:

I think the training helped us, as a program, to focus our efforts on student responsibility and accountability in a restorative setting rather than the more traditional punitive system. As for numbers, here are some I find interesting: Attendance has improved significantly. The last grading quarter of the previous school year we had 25 unexcused absences and 32 tardy incidents. The first quarter of this year we had four excused absences, one unexcused, and four tardy incidents.[8]

Over 50 percent of the elementary school students in Red Lake Falls, Minnesota, who were surveyed about their experiences with the Circle process indicated that:

- They get along better with their classmates,
- They feel better about themselves,
- They understand their classmate's feelings better,
- They can solve more of their own problems,
- Their daily school work improved,
- They feel that school is more fun, and
- They would like to see more circle sessions.[9]

Harnessing the attention and enthusiasm of adults and students is one of the promises of implementing restorative practices in the educational setting. When we respect everyone's ability in problem-solving activities,

7. Riestenberg, "Restorative Creativity," 1–2.

8. Ibid., 1.

9. Riestenberg, Restorative Schools Grants Final Report.

we take the first step toward creating a more peaceful, just, and productive school environment.

Workplace Circles

With organizations becoming such a large part of our lives, it is important to understand how they operate and the relationships of which they are composed, so we can better achieve our personal aspirations as we work with others to achieve the goals of the organization.

> At the same time our globe is "shrinking," our mobility is putting greater distance between us and our parents or grown children, between the places where we grew up and the places we now live, between ourselves and our friends from school. As these separations multiply, our hunger for community grows. So, too, does the time we devote to work. It is no wonder then that our organization becomes our second family—or at least the part of the organization in which we work. . . . An organization is not only a form of family, it is a form of community—a work community.[10]

Current organizational models were developed during the Industrial Age, which was characterized by mass production, centralized operations, control-and-command environments, and steep hierarchies in which a few individuals made decisions for the many people who did the work.

> Steep hierarchies result in the division of labor, the evolution of staff functions, and the development of "made up" career ladders, all of which contribute to fragmented organizations. In a fragmented organization, few people, if any, (1) can see the big picture—which means they understand organizational strategy, the work flows and processes, and their contribution to the finished product or service; (2) know how their interactions with co-workers and other work units support the success of the enterprise; or (3) have "line of sight," which means they understand the end user's requirements, the use of what is produced, and how their work contributes to customer satisfaction.[11]

We are now in the Electronic Communication Age, characterized by increased speed and content and, as information transfer becomes faster and work becomes seemingly less personal, the innate need for

10. Janov, *Inventive Organization*, 203.

11. Ibid., 91–92.

person-to-person contact becomes more important. This hunger for community includes being able to exchange ideas openly without fear of retribution, and being able to collaborate with coworkers in a safe and non-threatening environment.

There are many books in print about how to achieve a competitive advantage in business, with advice on such topics as: leading in a culture of change, strategies for organizational success, unleashing the power in your workforce, assuring high performance in an age of complexity, leading at the edge of chaos, and using the law for competitive advantage. Competition erects walls, however, and when it pervades all aspects of an organization's work it negatively impacts the one and only thing of true value in any organization—relationships.

As Jennifer Ball, Wayne Caldwell, and Kay Pranis state:

> Circles build communities; they provide support; they generate mutual understanding; they strengthen relationships; and they create spaces for healing and transformation. But what drew us as planners to the process most is their power to help people solve complex, emotionally charged, and often otherwise intractable problems.[12]

Instituting more layers of management, doing more strategic planning, and having more oversight and more regulation does not work. What works is a process that acknowledges the value of all participants, and that provides a non-judgmental space in which all voices can be listened to.

> One thing for sure, we need this Circle thing. This is the first time in twelve years at this plant that we've ever talked to each other. I mean really talked. This is the first time I'm getting to know people I've worked with for years. That cannot be a bad thing, and if it is, I say, let's have more bad things like this.[13]

> I hated meetings. I would miss as many as I could. I was always anxious to leave. Now I look forward to them, and I'm surprised how quickly the time goes by. Doing it in a Circle gives everyone a chance to have their say. We all learn more, and the stuff that comes out is the stuff that needs to come out to get at the real work we need to do with each other—to work with each other in a good way. The agenda is there, but it isn't the most important thing anymore. What is really important comes out, and it never

12. Ball et al., *Doing Democracy with Circles*, 3.
13. Pranis et al., *Peacemaking Circles*, 147.

did before. It stayed in the offices and in whispers. That's what made the meetings dishonest—and difficult. Well, sometimes it's difficult in Circles too, but in a different way. It's a good difficult, because it's honest and safe.[14]

The Circle process honors workers, and provides a forum in which they can make meaningful contributions that can, in turn, boost their self-esteem and their value as employees.

Circles in Civic Group Processes

Citizen Circles

A citizen is a person who holds himself accountable for the well-being of the entire community, chooses to own and exercise power rather than delegating it to others, and acknowledges that a community grows out of the *possibilities* of its citizens. The notion of *possibilities* removes the constraints of goals, objectives, and timelines; it envisions what citizens want their community to become, and how the gifts of every person can be utilized to fulfill that vision. *Possibilities* are not wishes, but rather declarations of what citizens are promising to accomplish by engaging, showing up, and exercising their citizenship responsibilities. The antithesis of being an active, responsible citizen is to choose to be a passive client of an external governing body—an organizational format that might sound familiar.

> Robert Putnam wrote *Bowling Alone* and amplified the conversation about the role that social capital plays in building community. As one part of his extensive research, he studied a fair number of Italian towns and tried to understand why some were more democratic, were more economically successful, had better health, and experienced better education achievement.
>
> His findings were startling, for he discovered that the one thing that distinguished the more successful from the less successful towns was the extent of social capital, or widespread relatedness that existed among its citizens. Success as a town was not dependent on the town's geography, history, economic base, cultural inheritance, or financial resources. . . . Community well-being simply had to do with the quality of the relationships, the cohesion that exists among its citizens. He calls this *social capital*. . . . Criminologists, for instance, have shown that the crime rate

14. Ibid., 235.

in a neighborhood is lowered when neighbors know one another well, benefiting even residents who are not themselves involved in neighborhood activities.[15]

The focus of Citizen Circles is on relationships. An important goal and outcome of the Circle process is encouraging healthy connections among groups of citizens, and between citizens and the community. Block introduces the terms "bonding social capital" and "bridging social capital" to describe the above connections. Recognizing that the well-being of each individual is directly connected to the well-being of others is essential to the success of communities. At the moment when people experience the fact that they can safely dissent or express doubts in Circles, and not lose their place in the community, they begin to join their community as full-fledged citizens. When citizen dissent is truly valued, the chance of citizens showing up as owners of the community goes up dramatically. Citizens who feel that their voices are listened to and valued become invested in their community and participate—not because of obligation, but because of desire. Collective-intelligence group solutions to problems always trump individual ones. Citizen Circles offer the opportunity to bring people who live on the fringes into the community.

> In fact, what distinguishes those on the margin in communities is they tragically live without real possibility. For many youth on the margin, the future is narrow, perhaps death or prison. They have trouble imagining a future distinct from the past or present. This is the real tragedy: not only that life is difficult, but that it is a life that holds no possibility for a different future.[16]

Citizen Circles offer the opportunity to make known the gifts of everyone, and to bring those gifts forward for the benefit of the community. Instead of labeling people on the fringes according to their deficits, it might be better to use terms such as "connector," "lights up the room," or "street-friendly." The Circle process ensures that all voices in the community are listened to, and that all ideas are given a fair hearing. Communities have a choice to either remain mired in a conversation about shortcomings, limitations, and problems to be solved or to move to a conversation of possibilities and ways to capitalize on the gifts of its citizens.

15. Block, *Community*, 17–18.
16. Ibid., 126.

Community action is often aimed at eliminating the sources of fear—neighborhoods are isolated or locked down, and more prisons are built. More protection is demanded, and increased funding for law enforcement is budgeted. We seem to be committed to doing more of what is not working.

In the town of Whitehorse in the Yukon, the existing jail was filled to capacity in 1993 and a new jail was being constructed. In 2003, ten years after the Circle process was introduced by Judge Barry Stuart, the original jail was filled to less than 50 percent of capacity and the new jail building was empty.[17]

> In Genese County, New York, where the community is involved in all aspects of the system, from attending to victim's needs to counseling offenders, the county jail population has been drastically reduced. Unlike other New York State county jails that run over 100 percent capacity, Genese County jails have rooms to spare.[18]

The above positive changes came about because citizens expressed their need to have change happen, and a forum was available in which their views could be listened to. Crime and disruption can be viewed as symptoms of the breakdown of relationships within a community. Involving the people who are close to those who have been harmed and to those who have caused harm significantly contributes to the success of restorative justice, and is essential to generating healing connections. The Circle process affords a good time and space in which relationships can be healed.

Community members have needs arising from crime, and they also have roles to play. Some people argue that when the state takes over in our name it undermines our sense of community. Communities are impacted by crime and should be considered to be stakeholders. Communities need attention to their concerns as victims.

> No one understands this more than Mike Butler, police chief of Longmont Colorado. One of Mike's favorite statements is: "for 80 percent of the calls we receive, people do not need a uniformed officer, they need a neighbor." Wise man.[19]

> Our prisons, our failure to adequately fund therapeutic measures for persons in emotional, mental or physical need, even the cries

17. Stuart, personal communication with author.
18. Stuart, *Building Community Justice Partnerships*, 13.
19. Block, *Community*, 132.

of opposition we are accustomed to hearing whenever a halfway house or group home is proposed for a residential neighborhood—all of these attempts to deny our responsibility suggest not dedication to the notion of a family of man but instead a readiness to discard those who disturb us. This is not the attitude that I see in Native communities today, and it is not the attitude they are attempting to foster. If nothing else, Native approaches may succeed in reminding us of how far we have strayed from notions of collective responsibility and the universal brotherhood of man.[20]

Citizen Circles do work, not only by addressing problems that arise, but also by providing a forum for designing a positive future community story. Encouraging community participation and changing the conversation from the past to the future is a powerful use of the Circle process, one that makes use of everyone's talents and gifts. Professionals are able to provide "services" such as counseling and addiction treatment, but citizen groups such as Community Circles are better able to deliver "care" to those who are in need.

Citizen Circles give people the chance to move beyond a set of community requirements to a consideration of their responsibilities, from thinking about leadership by a few to engagement by all, and from an attitude of aloofness to one of accountability and commitment. And all of the above positive outcomes are available at no cost except for the time required to advertise a Circle and arrange chairs.

The Wisdom of the Greek Agora

The agora of ancient Greece was a public place that was the focus of political, commercial, administrative, and social activity; the religious and cultural center; and the seat of justice. Citizen Circles provide such a forum—an agora—which is a good space for resolving difficult issues, for planning the future, and for strengthening relationships.

In the few years leading up to 2005, Chicago had built more than forty-five new branch libraries.[21] The Near North Branch was constructed at the boundary between two very different neighborhoods—the mainly white, wealthy Gold Coast along the shore of Lake Michigan, and Cabrini Green, with its predominantly African-American population living in pub-

20. Ross, *Dancing with a Ghost*, 161–62.
21. Putnam and Feldstein, *Better Together*.

lic housing. The library has Internet-connected computers and numerous community meeting rooms, and it contains local art, pictures of the schools in the neighborhoods, and books and magazines tailored to the languages and interests of the resident ethnic populations.

> On weekday afternoons, as many as seventy schoolchildren, most of them from Cabrini Green, fill the children's section. Some of them work with the volunteers in the Homework Help program, most of whom are Gold Coast residents, retirees looking for satisfying and interesting ways to stay connected with the world. . . . A woman who lives at a nearby mental health residence often spends hours in the library. Sometimes street people snooze at one of the tables, as welcome as anyone. . . . Before, I thought no one cared about people around Cabrini. And so we didn't care. Now I feel like someone is watching, trying to make things better. So I am trying to better myself and my children.[22]

Working together, the once hardline neighborhood boundary defined by ethnicity and economic differences has softened dramatically—to the benefit of all. The Chicago libraries have become a model for providing places where citizens can meet, interact, and put into practice the values of good citizenship. Circles, whether identified or recognized as such, can be agoras for a positive future and, as evidenced by Chicago's libraries, need only to be recognized, and convened.

The Near North Branch library is an agora—a safe meeting place, and a place where Citizen Circles comprising people of diverse backgrounds can learn from one another. It is a place where older people can use their experience to guide younger ones, and in which senior citizens are appreciated for the gifts that they willingly bestow. The value of senior citizens in the Near North Branch library parallels that of Native seniors in northern Ontario:

> They were revered not only for what they had done in the past but for what they could still do in the present. Even when their powers of observation began to fail, they possessed two things younger people lacked: a reservoir of experience [or, in the predictive enterprise, of memory-images], and sophisticated skills in pattern-thought which others were only developing. Because of those skills and attributes, older people remained of inestimable value long after their physical powers had deteriorated.[23]

22. Ibid., 36–37.
23. Ross, *Dancing with a Ghost*, 80.

Considerations in Planning Citizen Circles

Planning for Citizen Circles is important, and planning sessions can themselves be efficiently and effectively conducted in a Circle format. Some considerations are:

- What is the goal of the meeting?
- Whose voices should be heard? Are all interests represented? Who should be invited?
- What factors are relevant and must be considered?
- Who determines the discussion items?
- Who sets the rules and parameters for the discussion?
- If reaching a decision is a goal, how do we arrive at that decision?
- What Circle format would be best?
- What might go wrong?

Guidelines for Citizen Circles

It is important to agree on guidelines for the meeting, whether you are guiding a Circle or participating in it. Many meetings fail, and many valuable human resource hours are wasted, by not agreeing on guidelines. The following guidelines are good ones to consider:

- Agree on group values.
- Agree on the purpose for which the Circle is convened.
- Agree on guidelines for the Circle, including timing.
- Focus on issues, not personalities.
- Come to meetings prepared.
- Focus on the big picture.
- Bring your ideas, not your agendas.
- Listen to and value all opinions.
- Build on the positive points raised by others.
- Speak up on all matters of importance.
- Be honest.

The Circle Process in Civic Group Meetings—Democracy in Action

The title of this section includes the words "democracy in action," but the term "democracy" has come to mean different things to different people. In the experience of some, democracy is a process in which the people who speak the loudest win, or in which the people who have the most power, money, or privilege win. Majority rule is one strategy designed to approximate the ideal of democracy, but it does not ensure that everyone will be satisfied. When a majority of 51 percent "wins" and determines a group's future action, 49 percent of the participants are "losers" and will support the action only grudgingly.

The Circle process is democratic by design and, as such, has the potential to change the way in which organizations operate, and the way in which public meetings are conducted. Because conversation is regulated by the use of a talking piece, all participants have an equal chance to have their voice listened to, and all participants are able to focus on the words being spoken by others and the feelings expressed by them. All speakers are able to think through their thoughts, uninterrupted, and to present them without fear of being "cut off" or being "called down." All ideas are allowed to surface (including the "ridiculous" ones that later turn out to be valuable), and listeners have the opportunity to build on the positive points raised by previous speakers and to converge toward a group decision that meets the needs of all parties. Participants who are normally shy are bolstered, and talkative or boisterous participants are calmed because of the time-sharing guidelines agreed to at the start of the Circle.

Howard Vogel, with Hamline University's School of Law and Dispute Resolution Institute, argues that democracy might not be the invention of any one culture, but rather:

> "a natural response from a human impulse to be connected in a good way." . . . democracy moves us toward ideals of giving voice to those who have had no voice, engaging those who have been excluded, and empowering people to participate in making the decisions that affect their lives.[24]

Circles of almost any size can be accommodated. Most business groups will comprise no more than fifteen individuals, but citizen groups of up to sixty people who all want to have their "time in the sun" can benefit from the Circle process as well. There are some circumstances when

24. Ball et al., *Doing Democracy with Circles*, 9–10.

the Circle process would not be appropriate, and these occasions will be mentioned below. But let's focus for now on this new way of interacting with others—in a Circle format that values the input of all participants and permits difficult conversations to be held in a good way.

Many organizations are hierarchical and decisions are made at the top. We are culturally accustomed either to being told what to do (underlings) or telling others what to do (superiors). Someone is always in control. Top-down decision-making is an exclusionary process. The Circle process is inclusive, and shared leadership is a very important tenet. Use of a Circle approach tells participants that a decision has not already been made, and that it is not going to be made in a top-down manner. It sends a powerful message of respect for participants. For those in power positions, the equality of Circle participants may feel threatening. Leaders may find it hard to change their role from speakers to listeners, and from authority figures to equal participants. Non-leadership members of civic communities may not be accustomed to speaking in front of authority figures and being taken seriously.

Because values lie at the core of all group decisions, they should be clearly identified at the beginning of a Circle, and honored throughout. Do profits and power control decisions? Or do respect and fairness have a place in the decision-making process as well?

The Circle process recognizes the value of relationships. Yet, achieving a balance between building relationships and addressing issues/developing action plans goes against our training in Western culture. We are not accustomed to devoting time to building relationships and promoting mutual understanding. We want to be efficient and not "waste everyone's time." This explains why people new to the Circle process often feel pressure to get to the heart of things as quickly as possible. A key to successful Circle processes, and all meaningful interactions within groups, is relationship-building.

The Roles of Circle Keepers in Civic Group Processes:

- Help the group define overarching values,
- Help the group understand that relationship and identity issues underlie substantive issues;
- Help the group consider its work in terms of past, present, and future timeframes;

- Help the group clarify its goals and needs;
- Help the group understand its options;
- Summarize a group's progress;
- Help the group reach decisions, if such is a goal.

Group Decision-Making

Although this section focuses on civic gatherings, the comments apply equally to decision-making in Circles of all types and sizes. A good decision-making goal should be to arrive at an outcome that is both realistic and sustainable, and that everyone can live with. Some people avoid participation in meetings because they know from experience that their voices will not be listened to or acknowledged—except as a perfunctory show of "diversity" that carries little weight in decision-making. There is a better way.

The Circle process has the potential to change the way in which organizations operate and the way in which decisions are made. All democratic group decision-making processes strive for consensus. "Consensus decision-making" is a term that is mentioned often. Indeed, it is preferable to decisions made by fiat or by majority rule, but its implementation must be considered carefully. I define consensus to have occurred not when unanimous agreement has been reached, but when everyone has had a chance to voice their interests and needs, the options that have been defined are realistic, commitments match the resources available, and all participants can accept the plan even though some may disagree with parts of it. Participants are willing to accept and live with a decision and support it for the good of the group, even though it might not be the person's first choice.

The Circle process, with its multiple rounds of opportunities to talk without interruption, to be listened to and understood, and to ask questions, is a key to reaching consensus. It encourages all interests to be represented and respected; allows parties to deal directly with each other; provides equal and effective voice for all parties; creates a safe problem-solving environment that generates frank, honest, and respectful exchanges of fears, concerns, needs, and aspirations; and provides a forum for building relationships, forging new partnerships, and fostering cooperative, innovation problem-solving.

Circles shift our priorities from getting what we want as individuals to supporting each other as a community, so that we can all benefit. We may not all get everything we hope for. However, each participant can be assured that the outcome will balance everyone's interests in the best way possible—according to the collective wisdom of the group.

The consensus decision-making process that is used successfully by the Community Circles Board of Directors originated with the Quakers. All decisions are made by a "unified sense" of those present. "Unified sense" is defined as agreement by all participants that the course of action being considered is in the best interest of the group. Dissent by one or more individuals may be registered in one of two ways:

1. Standing aside: When an issue has been fully discussed and cannot be resolved by a unified sense of those present, the dissenting individual(s) may indicate that she/he is willing to stand aside and allow the proposal to be adopted. The unresolved concern is written down in the minutes, and becomes a part of the proposal.

2. Declaring a block: When an issue has been fully discussed and cannot be resolved by a unified sense of those present, the dissenting individual(s) may indicate that she/he chooses to block the proposal. The unresolved concern is written down and becomes a part of the minutes. Discussion of the issue continues.

The key to the success of Circle process decision-making is that everyone has a chance to tell their story, uninterrupted, and to have all others in attendance listen to that story and be able to ask clarifying questions to achieve a better understanding. The Circle process allows participants to build on good points mentioned by others, and to reach a group decision that would otherwise be impossible if each person's input had not been solicited.

The Circle process may take more time than decision-making per Robert's Rules of Order, but it ensures that everyone's voice is honored in the outcome.

When Is a Circle Process Appropriate and Not Appropriate?

I am grateful to Kay Pranis for raising my awareness of things that should be considered in planning Circles:[25]

25. Pranis, *Little Book of Circle Processes*, 50.

- Are there people who are willing to participate? Does the topic matter to anyone? If so, then the Circle process is appropriate.

- Would a meeting be valuable if it strengthened relationships, participants learned something of value, and people were able to discuss their gifts and offer them to others? If so, then the Circle process is appropriate.

- Would the input of others be meaningful? Would it have some role in the decision-making process? If so, then the Circle process is appropriate.

- Am I open to hearing and respecting perspectives very different from my own? If so, then the Circle process is appropriate.

- Is the intent to be respectful of all participants? If so, then the Circle process is appropriate.

- Am I (the leader or organizer) hoping to convince others of a particular point of view? Am I hoping only to change others? Do I have an agenda for the situation that I want the Circle to promote? If so, then the Circle process is *not* appropriate.

- Am I using a Circle only as a public relations strategy? If so, then the Circle process is *not* appropriate.

12

Community Circles—a Community Justice Initiative

BECAUSE THE CIRCLE PROCESS may be new to some readers, I choose to trace the development of Community Circles in Missoula, Montana, as one example of a community justice initiative.

Comments from Community Circles participants—both guests and supporters—are included to illustrate the positive impact that the Circle process can have on individuals and their families.

What Is Community Circles?

Community Circles is a program that places the primary responsibility for addressing family and community problems squarely on families and the community. Its basic principle is that healing relationships is a more fruitful way to develop peaceful, just, and productive communities than is punishment, and that dialogue is a better way to heal relationships than is reliance on debate.

Community Circles champions the Circle process and, by using it, provides a safe time and space in which people can express their needs, desires, and dreams in a caring environment. Community Circles recognizes that the Circle process has value both in repairing harm caused by misdeeds and in guiding people to interact more effectively in family, neighborhood, educational, civic, and business settings. The Community Circles Mission Statement is as follows:

> *The Community Circles program recognizes that the breakdown of relationships contributes to the breakdown of communities. We believe it is the responsibility of individuals and the community to heal these relationships in a way that maintains harmony and addresses difficult issues in a positive way. Honoring the ancient wisdom and*

practice of "Talking Circles," the volunteers of Community Circles
provide training in, and facilitation of positive, healing communica-
tions and listening skills for victims, offenders, and other individuals
and groups in conflict. Community Circles encourages those involved
to restore relationships and move forward toward a better life path,
while offering support for the journey.

Community Circles has been successful in helping many people and groups move to a better life path. We feel it is now timely to share our initial design, our growth path, where we are on our journey, and our aspirations and concerns, so that other individuals and groups can build on what we have learned, and new and even better programs can be brought to fruition. We offer our comments without hubris, in the knowledge that our growth has been by evolution rather than by design, and that we are continuing to learn each day. Our hope is that our words and ideas will spark a dialogue on how we can all contribute to the goal of achieving more collaborative human interactions. The comments below are not an exhaustive statement, and inquiries for more detailed information will gladly be fielded.

We are humbled by the wisdom of our indigenous forebears who, thousands of years ago, knew everything that the Community Circles program now encompasses. We stand honored to live in a time when dedicated people of exceptional intelligence and personal qualities have brought the precepts of restorative justice to the United States, and to other areas of the world. And we stand in debt to the many volunteers in Missoula, Montana, and throughout the world, who give of their time to listen patiently and to share openly from their own experience banks—in order to help people rebuild relationships that have been lost, damaged, or badly neglected.

A number of Circle processes—e.g., Family Group Conferencing—involve scripted procedures that ensure that the goals of the Circle process will be achieved—with typical goals being restitution and/or treatment plans. It's difficult to remember back to the first Circle held in the Community Circles program in 2002, but what seemed to be the right thing to do at that time was to proceed *without a script*. Our focus was, and continues to be, on giving participants a good space in which to tell their stories. Our Circles commonly begin with the simple question, "What's going on?" We engage in group exploration, and because we do not know the endpoint of any conversation, our format involves more risk than does one that uses a script. The reward we reap is that, by focusing on the stories of participants, we are constantly giving energy to them, and reinforcing their innate capacity to figure out how best to meet their own needs.

The Community Circles Journey

I first viewed the video *Circle Sentencing: A Yukon Justice Experiment* at the 1999 National Conference on Peacemaking and Conflict Resolution in Phoenix, Arizona. I was so stirred by the restorative justice message espoused by Judge Barry Stuart that I purchased the video and immediately began showing it to my mediation associates. I soon learned that Peacemaking Circles were being used in indigenous communities all across Canada, and that the Circle process had been introduced into the United States by Kay Pranis, who at the time was the Restorative Justice Planner for the Minnesota Department of Corrections. I contacted Kay and, with her counsel, life was breathed into Community Circles in 2002.

Since its incorporation as a non-profit organization, Community Circles has not only convened Circles on behalf of the court system, neighborhoods, families, and civic organizations, but has trained more than 160 individuals to be Circle Keepers in twelve communities across Montana.

Community Circles began as a volunteer-based, unfunded mandate, and it continues so today, with monetary contributions covering office supplies, volunteers providing administrative needs, and Circle meeting space provided free of charge by Common Quest Mediation, Inc. This low-budget, volunteer format has prevented us from doing all of the outreach that we would have liked to do, but the upside is that we have been able to weather economic downturns very well, and have been able to build a record of continuous service to the Missoula community. People continue to marvel when they learn that we do not charge for convening Circles for Missoula citizens, and that we are all volunteering our time and energy because of our belief in restorative justice and the Circle process.

Peter Block points to the work of David Bornstein, a journalist who has written about social innovations that have become large movements:

> Small scale, slow growth. Not one of the examples David describes began as a government or large-system-sponsored program. Each was begun with very little funding, no fanfare, and little concern about how to measure the outcomes. Each had a deeply committed and self-chosen leader with a commitment to make a difference in the lives of however many people they were able to reach.

Bornstein concluded that well-funded efforts, with clear outcomes, that spell out the steps to get there do not work. Changes that begin on a large scale, are initiated or imposed from the top, and are driven to produce quick wins inevitably produce few lasting results. . . .

If you reflect on the stories of the successful leaders who Bornstein documents, you realize that these entrepreneurs were committed enough and patient enough to give their projects time to evolve and find their own way of operating. . . .

It was after the model had evolved and succeeded on its own terms that it began to grow, gain attention, and achieve a level of scale that touched large numbers of people.

This means that sustainable changes in community occur locally on a small scale, happen slowly, and are initiated at the grassroots level.[1]

I was concerned during the formative days of the Community Circles program that we did not have small cohesive groups (clans, tribes) within which to convene Circles. After all, the Peacemaking Circles that work so well in indigenous cultures comprise people who have a communal history with one another. We *did* design the Community Circles program to include supporters, but I continued to have a sense of unease. It took me several years to finally come to grips with this issue, to realize that each time we convened a Circle we were helping individuals realize a *new* sense of community within their lives.

> To be honest I didn't have faith in this program. I never thought a group of strangers could help me at all. I was wrong. Community Circles is helpful in many ways! It helped me want to trust and listen cuz the people with C.C. do not judge and that's the most important thing of all. The program helped me want to fix my relationship w/ my brother. So if anyone has the chance to take this program then do it cuz it could be very helpful. (Community Circles guest)

The Objectives of Community Circles

The prime objective of Community Circles is to provide caring attention to members of the Missoula community who are in need—be they people who have been harmed, people who have caused harm, neighbors, or civic

---

1. Block, *Community*, 25–26.

or business entities. Within the overarching goal of helping to build a more peaceful, just, and productive Missoula community, the following specific objectives are in place:

- Empower families and community members to have voice in and shared responsibility for finding constructive resolutions to problems.
- Provide educational opportunities to learn about the power of the Circle process.
- Mentor new Circle groups in the development of their programs.
- Construct the foundation for better relationships among parties and within the community.
- Empower individuals and families to take more responsibility for decisions affecting their community.
- Help construct healing plans for affected parties.
- Build understanding, respect, and empathy for others.
- Identify, share, and promote community values.
- Identify measures to prevent future crimes or conflicts.
- Build community capacity for resolving future conflicts.
- Be available to Circle guests at any time in the future, and reconvene their Circle if they feel it would be beneficial to them.

> The program is very amazing in the sense of informalness and flexibility. There are no boundrys for subject matter and no primary focus on one person in the sense that everyone in the "circle" is thought of as equal and not labeled by the legal system with a "scarlet letter." (Community Circles guest)

Community Circles and the Formal Legal System

Police and the formal legal system have historically had the responsibility for maintaining harmony and managing conflict in the United States. Community justice initiatives shift some of the responsibility for resolving conflict from the state to communities and families, and in so doing they reinforce communities and families as the cornerstones of our society. The three quotations below are the words of Judge Barry Stuart, who worked for many years in the Canadian legal system and, while so serving, learned the value of restorative justice and the Circle process:

> The challenge is not to replace mainstream justice processes but to discover what they are best suited to do, how they can effectively work in partnership with other processes, and what conflicts are better served outside the formal justice processes.[2]

> *In each community a range of responses to crime is necessary.* At one end of the continuum, the formal adversarial legal system; at the other, the family, friends, and maybe a mediator or peacemaker negotiating a solution among all affected parties. . . . *We must create a better balance between what the state should and can do, and what family and communities should and can do. . . . The formal justice system must become what it was originally intended to be, a back-up to family and community processes for resolving conflict.*[3]

> We squander too many scarce resources, and fail to resolve too many conflicts by relying on only one process to deal with a diverse range of problems within communities.[4]

The Circle process affords an opportunity for the community to take charge of many of its own issues. Restorative justice and the Circle process humanize the harm caused by crimes or misdeeds, and help bring people together and rebuild relationships. The jobs of individuals working within formal legal systems are not threatened by the changes supported by Judge Stuart, but instead they may give people more satisfaction, as they witness the positive impact of the healing process and their roles in it. The formal legal system does contribute significantly to the community justice partnership by offering a clear alternative to an offender who chooses to no longer voluntarily participate in a Circle process.

> *This rather magical process encouraged an increased expression of self responsibility from my adult son. We came hoping for a solution to a practical problem and left with a gift of the circle truly seeing strength in my son. The practical problem remains but with more information than we had before. The re-frame is that there is a broader perspective and perhaps more hope than before despite*

2. Stuart, *Building Community Justice Partnerships*, 2.

3. Ibid., 3.

4. Ibid., 38.

considerable personal challenges. Thank you very much for this gift!
(Community Circles supporter)

I have been involved in many "traditional" group settings and none have ever allowed me the freedom to express myself and my views and to just generally be accepted for who I really am. This group was great, insightful, and fun. I was able to help out and support a coworker and that gave us an even better friendship. I am glad I was a part of it. (Community Circles supporter)

How Community Circles Can Contribute to Crime Prevention:

- Strengthening the ability of individuals, families, and the community to assume greater responsibility;
- Reconnecting people who have caused harm to positive environments within their families and communities;
- Rebuilding a sense of community;
- Surfacing the underlying causes of crime;
- Healing broken people and broken relationships.

The Community Justice System Vision

A community justice committee would be at the heart of a comprehensive community justice system.[5] A community justice system would contain a broad range of options, from informal police warnings to formal court hearings, and from community Circle processes to community input in court sentencing.

The community justice committee would field referrals from schools, police, victims, offenders, the courts, and citizens. Based on input from victims, offenders, and their families and supporters; from health, education, social services, and legal agencies; and from other community sources, the committee would suggest an option for resolution of the situation. Options might include police diversion, mediation, the formal court system, a facilitated Circle process such as Family Group Conferencing, and a community Circle process such as Community Circles. Community Circles, as one

5. Stuart, *Building Community Justice Partnerships*, 32–43.

example of a community justice initiative, would be a valuable component in such a community justice system.

> *Opened communication. I was skeptical at the beginning of both sessions but both times everyone had opened up and was willing to talk by the end.* (Community Circles guest)

Organizational Challenges

Internal

In all volunteer-based organizations, treating volunteers well is paramount. Honoring volunteers' expectations regarding their time commitment is crucial, and is done by announcing new opportunities in a timely manner, and by carefully matching Circle Keepers with opportunities. We periodically hold social evenings or dinners for Circle Keepers at a local restaurant, and often include a speaker from the Missoula community. If we don't hear from a Circle Keeper for a period of time, we call that person to see if they need support. We track Circle Keepers' changing life plans and monitor their desire to participate in more or fewer Circles, according to their professional and personal commitments.

Occasionally an obligation to Circle guests extends beyond the boundaries of the Circle process. We have transported parties to medical appointments, guided them through the maze of medical billing, attended high school graduations, and worked closely with probation officers when behavioral relapses occur. We constantly remain aware of the differences between what we offer and "counseling" or "therapy," and are always careful to honor the mandates of the formal legal system.

External

Sustaining a community justice initiative poses an enormous challenge. The challenge lies in providing a process that offers a better result at a lower transactional cost. It is a challenge that communities and law enforcement professionals cannot afford to avoid. The challenge lies not just in introducing a new process, but also in dealing with resistance to change and in motivating people to use and support new processes.

> *The enthusiasm to evaluate, especially to point out the failings of community justice initiatives by government researchers, by academics, and by the media, is surprising, given the absence of the same energy to critically assess the overall prudence of annual investment in the formal justice system.*[6]

For the community justice partnerships to evolve, justice partners must be innovative in developing new processes that retain the essence of fundamental principles of justice. There is nothing sacred in existing justice practices or procedures. It is the integrity of the principles, not current practices and procedures, that must be retained. To the extent these practices and procedures can be altered without diminishing fundamental principles to accommodate the needs of communities—they should be.[7]

The primary successes of community justice initiatives are not readily measurable. Their important contributions flow chiefly from secondary impacts that prevent crime, and prevent conflicts from evolving or exploding into crime.

> The persistence of serious crime, coupled with the important, but often intangible success of community justice, poses a dilemma for community justice. A similar dilemma confronts medical practitioners working in preventive medicine. Medical professionals involved in preventive medicine struggle vainly for appropriate funding, competing with colleagues with ready public support for their higher profile work in crisis treatment. So it will be with community justice. The preventive work of community justice, despite its valuable contribution to society, will not attract the same funding support from government as justice agencies responding to high-profile crime.[8]

It is easy to become enamored with linear processes that start with a defined problem—for example, grafitti on a wall. In this case, the process brings the owner of the wall and the perpetrator together, and designates a time line for measuring fulfillment of the imposed corrective action. Such victim-offender processes are, indeed, valuable, and have helped in the resolution of many issues. I am a victim-offender mediator and have trained many people in this valuable process; I support it heartily. In our results-oriented society that relies on metrics for program support and

6. Ibid., 26.
7. Ibid., 28.
8. Ibid., 28–29.

funding, it is harder to convince people of the value of a Circle process that provides a safe and confidential place in which people can talk, be listened to, and can work toward their own resolution of their problems—and grow by so doing.

I have voiced the metaphor "large ships turn slowly" to many peers over the years; when doing so recently to an associate in Hawai'i, the response was, "We have a lot of those large boats here in Hawai'i, and worse, many are stuck on the reef too."

> I thought that community circles was a great way to interact with the ideas and feelings of others, Although some may not agree with others, but it is agreed not to be judgemental and speak your mind every time. It is important to take into consideration another person's point of view; for it might just help in the long run of a certain situation. Thank you for the help in new ways to discover the thousands of possibilities. (Community Circles guest)

Core Procedural Elements of Community Circles

Core elements—holding orientation Circles, reporting to referring agencies, following up with guests after their scheduled number of Circle conferences, and consensus decision-making—have been addressed above.

Partnerships and referrals are also important core elements, and merit special mention. There is no disagreement that there is an increasing need in our society to provide confidential and safe spaces in which people can talk about issues of importance to them. We also know that there are willing volunteers in all of our communities who are eager to extend a caring hand to fellow citizens who are hurting—both those who have been harmed and those who have caused harm. The obvious link between the needs and the willing providers, then, is partnerships with groups that are aware of the need and are willing to make referrals. For example, a judge in Missoula saw the Circle process as a way to decrease the number of "frequent flyers" in her court, and a probation officer saw the Circle process as a good way for adult felons to reintegrate into the Missoula community.

We have found that personal contact with people in the court system, law enforcement officers, government officials, neighborhood leaders, social service providers, and teachers and school administrators is the most effective way in which to generate referrals. We place our brochure in prominent locations throughout the community, and we have made many presentations at civic luncheons. We have chosen not to advertise with print, radio, billboard, or TV ads, but this approach might be considered. As with all advertising, measuring success relative to dollars and energy expended is a challenge.

> *Our blended, fractured, and stressed-out family is much stronger and kinder as a result of participating in the Circle.* (Community Circles guest)

> *Community Circles has truly been a positive experience for my family. We have watched our daughter struggle for many years and we have attended a variety of family counseling sessions. This was one of the most positive experiences and was very helpful in learning some new communication skills. The volunteers are wonderful, caring people who were very encouraging and provided a safe, comfortable environment to share.* (Community Circles supporter)

The Importance of Confidentiality

The Community Circles confidentiality requirement allows participants to speak freely—often about things never before mentioned. It provides a safe space for people to talk openly about difficult issues such as past misdeeds, embarrassing current situations, painful family relationships, anxieties, or needs and aspirations. To properly uphold our Community Circles commitment to "do no harm" and to also acknowledge our role as a partner with the formal legal system, we require all participants to sign the following confidentiality agreement:

> *It is understood that Circle conferences are most productive if open and honest communications can be assured. Accordingly, we agree that notes and oral communications made during the course of this Circle conference are confidential, unless all participants agree to proceed otherwise. Further, it is the responsibility of Circle Keepers to report the following out of the Circle:*
>
> - *A threat of harm to self or others will be reported to the proper authority.*
>
> - *If a client in a Circle conference mentions a violation of probation by substance use, the Circle Keepers will tell the client to self-report, stressing the benefit of honesty. The Circle Keeper has the option to contact the appropriate authority and recommend*

a "progressive discipline" response. If the client chooses not to self-report, the Circle process will be terminated.

- If a client appears to be under the influence of an illicit substance when appearing for a Circle conference, the Circle Keepers will terminate the Circle process and report to the appropriate authority.

Circle Keeper Training Protocol

All segments of Community Circles training seminars are conducted in a Circle format. Our standard training seminar is two days long, with emphasis on experiential learning and providing ample time for development of openness, trust, and camaraderie. We have conducted one-day training seminars, but that format cuts short the time for practice scenarios, and is not recommended. Comprehensive manuals are delivered to each attendee a week before the seminar, so that we can make good use of our time together during the seminar.

The initial Circle on the first day is designed for introductions, setting expectations, and agreeing on guidelines. Special needs of attendees—such as hearing weakness—are identified so that participants can plan their actions accordingly. The expectations and guidelines are listed on easel pads, with a third easel pad posted for participants to make notes of questions at any time they come to mind. We call this easel pad "The Parking Lot." Following introductions, the group is immediately immersed in a training scenario—with roles assigned, and with two of the trainers being the Circle Keepers. The lead Circle Keeper opens the Circle, guides it, and closes it after a set amount of time. The second Circle Keeper leads a debrief discussion of the scenario, so that feelings can be shared and questions fielded. Following lunch, an overview of the Circle process is presented, and the group is immersed in two more training scenarios—with participants being the Circle Keepers, and the trainers being mentors or process guides. Homework at the end of the first day consists of asking each participant to prepare a practice scenario based on their own experience.

The morning of the second day begins with a check-in Circle, followed by presentations of the homework scenarios, and a decision by the group of the three scenarios that will be used during the day. One such real-life scenario brought forward by a participant—one that I remember well—is as follows:

Grandpa is in the hospital, unconscious, and with very little time to live. During his lifetime, Grandpa made it clear that he was not, and never would be, a religious person. Grandma, on the other hand, is very religious. She is in the early stages of dementia and is often disoriented and forgetful. Though her mind may falter, she remains committed to her religion, and believes that it is necessary for the Church to administer last rites to her husband so that she and Grandpa will share eternity in heaven. The participants in the Circle were Grandma, her daughter, a granddaughter, a son-in-law, the family doctor, and a church support person.

After a ninety-minute-long Circle, no conclusion had been reached, but the person who had submitted the scenario was grateful for having gained new understanding, and for having heard new approaches to the situation.

Following two morning practice scenarios and debrief discussions, and during lunch, one of two videos—*Circle Sentencing: A Yukon Justice Experiment,* or *Circles. It's About Justice. It's About Healing.*—is shown, and discussion entertained. The first afternoon time block includes the third real-life scenario, followed by a scenario debrief and a discussion of the entire training experience. A closing exercise involves giving everyone a virtual backpack that is filled with all of the "stuff" that burdens our everyday lives. The question is then posed: What are you willing to take out of your backpack in order to make room for two of the new tools you have learned about during our time together? The comments offered have been wonderfully thoughtful.

Expectations, as listed on the easel pad, are reviewed, and the items in "The Parking Lot" are addressed and resolved. Evaluation forms are distributed and completed, and a closing Circle is held, during which time participants are invited to share their reflections about their Circle training experience.

Measuring Success

Some standard ways in which to measure a program's success are (1) by continuity and (2) by community acceptance. Community Circles has been offering the Circle process to Missoula citizens for more than thirteen years, and is accepted as a meaningful program in the Missoula community.

At the end of each Circle process (two or more Circle conferences), we offer guests an opportunity to write comments about their experience. Our file is replete with positive comments, and we use them, without attribution, when we reach out to groups in the Missoula community. A comment from one of our Circle guests that speaks to the need for more outreach is telling:

> *This program offers a really great alternative to those individuals who need a jump start after making mistakes in life. I liked the Circle because it teaches folks that there are many other options available in the community to ask for assistance. A lot of individuals would offer support, I believe, if they knew how well this program works.* (Community Circles guest)

In our twenty-first century, metric-focused environment, in which the term "evidence-based" is almost a mantra, testimonials are a strong but insufficient basis for garnering future support. The rate of recidivism of people who have completed their commitment to the court is often used as a measure of the value of community justice initiatives such as Community Circles. If a person does, indeed, relapse, but does so less frequently than before involvement in a healing program, is this not a worthy accomplishment? If a medical procedure fails to work as well as anticipated, do doctors give up, or do they keep trying to find a good answer?

Rupert Ross states:

> In dealing with people who have been less than successful in resisting their weaknesses, we often think of punishment as a first response. Native people, on the other hand, traditionally saw each person as essentially good, provided regular healing assistance and, when problems nevertheless remained, thought first in terms of further help. . . . We react to crime by ostracizing the offender in jail, while they view social and spiritual estrangement as the cause of the crime.[9]

It is a challenge to develop forward-focused, evidence-based programs that can be evaluated statistically. We designed such a program in collaboration with two professors at the University of Montana. Partnership with a court in Missoula that handles underage drinking violations has been sought, but not yet achieved. Such a program would be a way to quantitatively document the value of the Community Circles community justice initiative in addressing a serious community problem that is costing

---

9. Ross, *Dancing with a Ghost*, 180–81.

many lives and dollars. We are hopeful that such a partnership can yet be formed.

Work conducted by the Washington State Institute for Public Policy (WSIPP) can provide a blueprint for designing and executing an evidence-based evaluation program. A WSIPP report published in 2004 specifically addresses program design and evaluation. A summary of this work follows.

> In 1997, the Washington State legislature passed the Community Juvenile Accountability Act (CJAA). The primary goal of the CJAA is to reduce juvenile crime, cost effectively, by establishing "research-based" programs in the state's juvenile courts. The basic idea is straightforward: taxpayers are better off if their dollars fund programs that have been proven to be effective in achieving key policy outcomes, in this case re-offending.
>
> The CJAA funded the nation's first statewide experiment concerning research-based programs for juvenile justice. Because selected treatment programs had already been researched elsewhere in the United States, usually as small-scale pilot programs, the question here was whether they work when applied statewide in a "real world" setting. This report indicates that the answer to this question is yes—when the programs are competently delivered.
>
> The basic findings are these:
>
> 1. When Functional Family Therapy (FFT) is delivered competently, the program reduces felony recidivism by 38 percent. The cost-benefit analyses find that FFT generates $2.77 in savings (avoided crime costs) for each taxpayer dollar spent on the program, regardless of therapist competence. For competent FFT therapists, the savings are greater—$10.69 in benefits for each taxpayer dollar spent.
>
> 2. When competently delivered, Aggression Replacement Training (ART) has positive outcomes with estimated reductions in 18-month felony recidivism of 24 percent and a benefit to cost ratio of $11.66.
>
> 3. The Coordination of Services program achieved a decrease in 12-month felony recidivism, and the estimated benefit to cost ratio is $7.89.
>
> 4. Because of problems implementing the Institute's evaluation design, no findings are associated with Multi-Systemic Therapy (MST). If the courts and the state wish to continue funding MST, the Institute recommends re-evaluating the program.

These findings affirm the merit of the legislature's investment in research-based programs for juvenile offenders. The next step is to implement the CJAA quality assurance standards so taxpayers can fully benefit from these programs.[10]

Because the WSIPP "Coordination of Services" program most closely matches the work of Community Circles, additional information from the 2004 report is included:

> Coordination of Services (COS), developed by Patrick Tolan, Ph.D., provides an educational program to low-risk juvenile offenders and their parents. The goals of COS are to describe the consequences of continued delinquent behavior, stimulate goal setting, review the strengths of the youth and family, and explain what resources are available for helping to achieve a positive, pro-social future for the youth. . . . COS was implemented in the Snohomish County Juvenile Court and called the "Way Out" program. . . . The following are key features of Way Out:
>
> - Low-risk juvenile offenders are court-mandated to attend, thus assuring a captive audience of youth who are at a crossroads when early intervention can make a difference.
>
> - Parents/guardians are also required to attend, thus providing an opportunity to teach parent and child the same skills simultaneously. Additionally, the participants are given a vehicle to open lines of communication and make shifts in thinking.
>
> - Community groups present participants with information concerning the services they provide.[11]

Success of the Circle process is perhaps best evidenced by its impact on each individual's life. A few years ago, we met four times with a sixteen-year-old girl who had been referred to Community Circles for multiple "minor in possession" offenses. By the end of the fourth Circle conference, we had all shared the ups and downs of our lives and had developed a friendship with each other. At the start of the closing round of the talking piece, I suggested that we each consider telling the guest something positive that we had learned about her. When the talking piece reached the girl, she broke down in tears, and said that nobody had *ever* said anything positive about her. It's difficult to quantify such experiences, but I like to think that

---

10. WSIPP, *Outcome Evaluation*, 1.

11. Ibid, 12.

the Circle process gave that teenager a much-needed boost on her path to responsible adulthood.

> *I am pleased with the process of the Circles program. My son was at a place where he was under so many bad choices that he didn't know how to move forward. Not only did the Circles program give him a positive outlook on life, it gave the two of us a place to touch base during a very busy, chaotic time in our lives. I know that my son now has wonderful people to touch base with and can leave the State knowing he will be alright. Thank you. (Community Circles supporter)*

Aspirations

The potential for expanding the use of the Circle process is limited only by people's awareness of the process, their creativity, and their desire to create a better world. With awareness, the Circle process can have value every day—in relationships between relatives, neighbors, business associates, elected officials, states, and countries. One important application of the Circle process in the future could be in resolving so-called intractable disputes—both domestically and internationally. From our experience in Community Circles, we *know* what can happen when you give people the opportunity to talk, uninterrupted, and when you provide a good time and space in which people can listen with the intent of understanding.

One theme of the current treatise has been that life's interactions are not linear, and that attempts to treat them as such are a disservice to the possibilities within each human being. In keeping with this theme, the aspiration of Community Circles is to continue providing time and space for people to tell their stories and, by so doing, to gain strength for their life journeys.

> *Community Circles program has given me a whole new outlook on life. Not only the problems I had with the law were talked about but also my personal problems. We discussed the good and important things in my life and talked about ways to improve. My supporters were amazing. Their storys about their struggles and hard times has given me inspiration to get my act straight together now before I get in a hole that I can't get out of. I believe that Community Circles program is an inspiration place that more peopel who are getting in*

troubel should go to discuss there problems, what's making them get in troubel. (Community Circles guest)

Summary

Community Circles is an emergent community justice initiative and, as such, the information offered above is a progress report. Community Circles has evolved by experimentation and thoughtful listening. If the description of our journey has value for any like-minded individuals or groups, great. We will look forward to learning from everyone who is on the restorative justice path.

Perhaps the best way to summarize the Community Circles program is to quote the two phases we have heard repeatedly from our guests and their supporters:

"I can't believe you are volunteering your time to listen to my story."

"It's so nice to be in a non-judgmental space."

13
The Opportunity

THE CIRCLE PROCESS IS a powerful tool for resolving problems, based on:
(1) cooperation, (2) achieving strong relationships and positive interactions
with one another, (3) focusing on the gifts of individuals, and (4) building
communities in which people want to live. The Circle process has worked
well for thousands of years, and embodies the promise that the future can
be bright for those individuals and groups willing to embrace it.

The Promise of Cooperation

We *can* change the culture of competition to one of cooperation. Cooperation tears down walls, treats people as unique and valuable individuals,
builds relationships, and encourages group solutions based on the experiences, talents, and creative ideas of all participants. Cooperation is a compassionate way to go through life, and its value is supported in studies of
human interactions in many cultures. Alfie Kohn reminds us:

> Seven different studies, then, with vastly different populations and
> measures of success, have all determined that intentional competi-
> tion is associated with lower performance.[1]

> Competitiveness . . . creates easily aroused envy towards the stron-
> ger ones, contempt for the weaker, distrust toward everyone . . .
> so the satisfaction and reassurance which one can get out of hu-
> man relations are limited and the individual becomes more or less
> emotionally isolated.[2]

> When we cooperate, we are inclined to like each other more. . . .
> cooperation teaches us, more broadly, the value of relationship.

1. Kohn, *No Contest*, 53.
2. Ibid., 140-41.

Cooperation means that the success of each participant is linked to that of every other. This structure tends to lead to mutual assistance and support, which, in turn, predisposes cooperators to feel an affinity for one another. At the very least, cooperation offers an *opportunity* to interact positively (which independent effort does not and which competition actively discourages); at the most, it provides an irresistible *inducement* to do so.[3]

Whereas competition creates an atmosphere of hostility and does nothing to overcome differences, cooperation builds bridges. Its capacity for encouraging positive regard is no less potent when the cooperators are from different backgrounds, as the studies show quite clearly. . . . the texture of our relationships depends to a significant degree on the context in which we come to know each other. I will look very different to someone for whom I am a rival than to someone for whom I am a partner.[4]

The Circle process is a cooperative activity that builds on the strengths of all participants. The Circle process supports group efforts to build on the positive thoughts and ideas of others—in the search for answers that are the keystone to building peaceful, just, and productive communities. The Circle process asks the question, "How are we going to act together?"

The Promise of Strong, Enduring Relationships

We *can* develop strong and enduring relationships within our families, neighborhoods, and civic and business associations. By devoting time and energy to listening to the stories of family members, friends, and associates, we will not only gain an educational opportunity, but will build strong bonds within groups and solid bridges between groups. Relationships that are built on caring actions are lasting ones that provide bountiful rewards. The democratic Circle process has a proven record for improving relationships in all situations in which Circles have been convened.

The Promise of Positive and Rewarding Communication Patterns

We *can* change the destructive debate paradigm to one based on dialogue, and we *can* focus our conversations on capabilities, gifts, and hope instead

3. Ibid., 149.
4. Ibid., 151.

of on deficiencies, faults, and fear. Positive communication patterns allow people to deal with conflict in a way that resolves difficulties and builds respect. The Circle process offers the opportunity for groups to move from the current dominant win-lose model of interaction to a consensus model in which nobody loses anything of significant value.

The Promise of Healing as an Alternative to Punishment

We *can* help people move toward better life paths, by listening to their needs, desires and dreams, and by guiding them based on our Circle Keeper experience banks.

The Circle process, based on the principles of listening and caring, is ideally suited to providing individuals with the time and space to climb out of the hole they are in, gain strength in their innate abilities, develop confidence, learn the tools that will make them successful, and move forward to a better life path. The biggest gift that the Circle process offers is: hope. Without it, nothing is possible; with it, the world becomes a cornucopia of possibilities. The healing Circle approach has been proven in indigenous cultures, and it can work in the United States in the twenty-first century.

The Promise of Peaceful, Just, and Productive Communities

We *can* accept and act on our responsibilities as citizens to resolve many of our own community difficulties. We *can* change the dominant model for dealing with wrongdoers, from punishing them to healing them, and welcoming them back into our communities. We *can* recognize the strengths of all citizens, and build on those strengths to achieve the possibilities that are waiting to be discovered.

The Circle process provides a key to developing communities in which safety is a given, citizens participate because they know that their voices will be listened to, and in which they are valued for the gifts they can provide toward building the peaceful, just, and productive citizen interactions that we all desire.

The Magic of the Circle Process

The Circle Keepers in the Community Circles program commonly voice the word "magic" during debrief meetings. We have never been able to accurately define the word, but have always reached agreement on the feeling experienced by our guests and by us. Perhaps the best way to evoke the magic of the Circle process is to think of the feeling you have when you have provided a safe space for people to tell their story, been a caring listener, and witnessed a positive change in the mien of the person or group for whom the Circle has been convened. We often avoid using the term "magic" in communication with people not familiar with the Circle process, for fear of being viewed as disconnected from the real world. The magic that happens in Circles is, however, very solidly tethered to the real world, and those of us who have experienced that magic are committed to sharing it whenever we can.

14
The Challenge

THIS CHAPTER IS THE most difficult one to write. To merely summarize the thoughts and ideas that have been presented above would be to caste aspersions on the reader's intelligence. And to offer suggestions would be to preach without intent to do so. With those caveats, we'll begin with a quotation from Buckminster Fuller, and then proceed with a few personal comments—some of which derive from my background in teaching communications—with the thought that they might be helpful.

> You never change things by fighting the existing reality. To change something, build a new model that makes the existing model obsolete.[1]

Designing a Future Worthy of Our Intelligence

This overarching challenge is a daunting one, but also one that can be accomplished if each of us commits to doing a small part of the work—in our personal lives and in our interactions with family members, neighbors, and civic and business partners. The challenge is to relearn how to use the tremendous power of the human mind in order to live with each other and with our environment in peaceful, cooperative, and supportive relationships. The circle process is a proven tool for helping meet this challenge.

One of the specific challenges we face is moving from a competitive to a cooperative way of interacting with one another. We can do so by clearly stating our feelings and our perception of facts, acknowledging that we have a limited perspective and asking for help in understanding issues better. Our focus can be on understanding situations better rather than on winning prizes.

1. Quoted in Quinn, *Beyond Civilization*, 137.

Another challenge is to change from focusing on people's deficits and past wrongdoings to focusing on their strengths. Consciously giving energy to each person with whom we come in contact is a positive step that will impact a great number of people. Conversations that focus on gifts and possibilities, as opposed to what *cannot* be accomplished because of real or perceived constraints, can be the start of citizen involvement and positive community development. Citizenship involves moving from passive submission to involvement, from merely fulfilling requirements to taking responsibility, to making a commitment to the whole—to the entire community.

Changing the punishment-based formal legal system is, again, a daunting challenge. The information presented in this book documents alternatives to retribution that have been used successfully for thousands of years. Our challenge is to speak out in favor of healing as a positive way to address wrongdoing, and also as a way to capitalize on the gifts that each individual has within them.

Dedicating time to telling and listening to stories—in families, neighborhoods, and civic and business groups—is crucial not only to solving the problems of life, but also to capitalizing on learning opportunities. When people mention the need for "speed, practicality, and efficiency" in meetings, recognize these words as code for keeping the current system in place. Maintaining the status quo eliminates any possibility for harvesting new ideas that sprout in creative spaces.

Although people want desperately to take uncertainty out of the future, its removal constrains the future to being merely a remake of the past. Our challenge is to embrace the mystery and uncertainty of the future, to learn from our missteps, and to build on the wild and crazy ideas of everyone involved—without concern for personal acknowledgment or praise.

A meaningful manner in which to capture the essence of our challenges is to learn the ways of our indigenous brothers and sisters—ways that have worked well for thousands of years—and apply them to the dynamic environment of the twenty-first century.

The Importance of Positive Communication Patterns

A focus of this book is on the importance of relationships—for resolving conflicts, and for designing good personal and community futures. Good relationships rely on positive communication patterns and, because of the great importance of verbal communication, the following ideas are offered for consideration.

Be Aware of Using Value-Laden, Judgmental Labels

Be aware of the use of value-laden, judgmental labels—labels that have the potential to foment destructive, competitive attitudes and behaviors. Such labels highlight the characteristics of people at the expense of understanding the relationships between them. They rank people as being either better or worse, and give rise to power hierarchies and the potential for abuse of that power. They divide people into polarized camps. How often does each of us apply judgmental labels that establish a hierarchy—in which the labeled person is considered to be of a lower rank than ourselves? Do we ever invent hierarchies where none exist? And does hierarchical thinking based on title or power dictate what we see and how we respond to what we see?

Awareness of the damage inflicted by the intentional or unintentional use of judgmental labels can be a powerful tool for promoting effective collaboration between individuals and groups. At a time in our society when it is important to bring people and groups closer together for the purpose of addressing important problems, a better understanding of the negative impact of value-laden judgmental labeling is a worthwhile goal.

Avoid the Trap of Implied Judgment

Value-laden, judgmental nouns and adjectives are relatively easy to recognize—once we develop an awareness of them. More insidious, however, are implied judgmental words that often masquerade as sarcasm. The following phrases have the same potential as direct judgmental words to polarize and harm relationships:

- "Jim's really nice. He's not nearly as boring as your last boyfriend." (You have a bad taste in companions.)

- "Your presentation was fantastic. It was much easier to follow than your last one." (Your last presentation was really bad.)

- "Susie, you ski really well—almost as good as a man." (gender judgment)

- "You should have . . ." (I obviously know better than you.)

Awareness of implied judgmental words and phrases can preserve friendships and smooth interactions within communities.

Stay Cool When Someone Labels You

If you feel that someone is deliberately applying a judgmental label to you, they have probably hit one of your "hot buttons." You have options: you could either choose to escalate the situation by applying a judgmental label in return, knowing that you would be hurting the relationship; or you could retreat and make no response at all, realizing that you would be choosing a destructive avoidance path that will also negatively impact the relationship.

A third option is available: be silent for a minute or two, and metaphorically "paddle into an eddy" so you don't say something or do something that you might later regret. Your silence will let the other person know that you value what has been said, and that you want your response to be well thought out and equally valued when it is received. When the conversation begins again, a simple statement of your feelings is a good way to proceed.

Your companion probably has no clue about the negative impact of judgmental labeling, so why not spread the word by offering the following: "You know, the judgmental label you just applied to me felt like a put-down, and it made me feel really rotten. Did you mean to have that effect on me?" Ninety-nine percent of the time, the other person will say "no". What a simple and valuable communication tool!

Resist the Need to Respond

When we are asked for our opinion, consider responding in a way that invites the questioner to say more about *their* view of the situation. The following approaches are worthy of consideration:

- "One way to look at it might be . . ."
- "I feel . . ."
- "This is just my opinion, and I realize that everyone saw the performance from a different perspective, but I felt that . . ."
- "That's a good question. I'll have to think about it for awhile . . ."
- "What do the rest of you feel?"

The respect that the other party will feel you have given them, and the potential for a meaningful dialogue as opposed to an adversarial debate, will be rewarding.

Ask Yourself a Question When You Have an Urge to Make a Judgmental Statement

When you would ordinarily voice a value-laden, judgmental label—such as "He's disgusting"—consider instead asking yourself a few questions:

- What was it he did that made me feel this way?
- What's going on that has changed our relationship?
- How might I have some responsibility for the current situation?

Consider Saying "I Feel . . ." Instead of "It Is . . ."

Instead of stating, "That lecture really sucked," consider saying, " I didn't get very much out of the way he presented the material. At least that's the way I feel right now. What's your take on it?" When we express our feelings, we leave the door open to the possibility that other people might see the world differently, and we also open the door to learning from diverse viewpoints. There is no such thing as an invalid feeling. Answers stated with certainty, however, often end up being ammunition for polarization, argument, or damage to relationships.

Deal with Rumors in a Positive Way

Rumors are statements that have passed through numerous mouths and ears. If a rumor impacts you and makes you feel defensive (read competitive), the best way in which to de-fuse it is to clarify the source, and determine first-hand the verity of the information.

Do Not Give Unsolicited Advice

If you ask someone for advice, feedback, or constructive input, you are giving that person a signal that you respect them and want to learn from their expertise and experience. If someone gives you advice, feedback, or input *without* your invitation, they are doing so from an implied level of superiority—based on their opinion of your needs and your capability to address those needs. It is valid in such circumstances to ask yourself, "Are they fulfilling my needs or theirs?"

Give Energy Whenever Possible

Practice saying, "I hear what you're saying [acknowledgment], *and* . . ." rather than, "I hear what you're saying, *but* . . ." Take every opportunity to build on positive points raised by others. This approach works well in conversations with one other person and in larger gatherings. It offers an opportunity to not only give energy to others, but to learn by so doing.

I heard the term "emotion contagion" recently, and consider it to be a good way in which to view the positive impact that you can have on family members, friends, and associates by using positive communication patterns.

15
The Risks

The Risks of Taking Action

THE RISKS OF EMBRACING and acting on the ideas in this book include being called down and ostracized for your efforts—by those individuals who have invested their careers in competitive pursuits. The benefits of participation in the restorative justice journey do not lend themselves easily to quantification, and are seldom blared in newspaper headlines. More commonly, they reside in the personal knowledge that you have cared for and offered guidance to an individual or group in need on their journey to a better life path. Patience is required to change a system of community interaction that has relied for many years on competitive debate. Those people who are accustomed to top-down community leadership, or who have found comfort from being either at the top or somewhere below, may find it difficult to accept a new and more productive type of participatory citizenship.

Creativity exists at the edge of chaos, and the formal legal system and many entrenched civic and business organizations loath chaos. The risk of embarking on a creative design journey into unknown waters is not for the faint of heart, and those individuals who agree to the journey should do so knowingly. The challenge of spreading a new culture is a hearty one, and acting on new ideas is a risk that will take energy and perseverance. At times, the uphill hike will be very tiring, and companions will be valuable. Involving other courageous individuals with you—who believe in restorative justice and the Circle process—is a good way for all of us to reach a meaningful "tipping point."[1]

---

1. Gladwell, *Tipping Point*.

The Risks of Inaction

The dominant way in which violations of the law and of community expectations are addressed in our culture is unsustainable. The costs are obscenely high in terms of dollars spent, lives warehoused, and human potential squandered. If we choose to do nothing, the number of criminals in the United States will continue to grow, and the need for larger and more secure holding facilities will continue to usurp more of our resources.

The ways in which we communicate with one another, and in which we teach our children to communicate, in the pursuit of resolving problems and designing the future, are severely lacking. If we choose to do nothing, our community interactions will continue to breed frustration, our educational facilities and programs will wilt, and our communities will languish. The risk of being a silent member in a society that is on a negative track is that we will watch the status quo continue to unfold—when a positive contribution could have been made. If we choose to do nothing, the future will indeed be a remake of the past.

All of the above consequences of inaction are unacceptable within the true meaning of citizenship. Restorative justice, and the Circle process within it, are tools for achieving a positive future of our making, for bringing citizenship back to a position of respectability, and for achieving the peaceful, just, and productive communities that we crave.

16
What Does Success Look Like?

SOME OF YOU HAVE now been introduced to restorative justice and to the Circle process for the first time; others of you have had an opportunity to consider them more deeply and to reflect on their meaning in your own lives. Whether circular or rectangular, and real or mere mathematical constructs, Circles are a powerful symbol for times and places where people can gather to share their needs, desires, and dreams; have difficult conversations; and define themselves as a community. Circles are places where democracy can be enacted and made real. Circles are the canvases on which our lives and community stories can be painted. They are safe places within which joys can be voiced, tears shed, questions asked, and new ideas brought forward without fear of ridicule—in which citizens can bond together, and build bridges to those with different views.

The terms "peaceful" and "productive" capture the qualities of a community in which justice includes everyone, positive energy resides within and radiates outward with each interaction, and people voluntarily engage with and care for each other. Peaceful and productive communities are ones in which people are treated with respect, citizens work together to resolve difficulties, and people help others to achieve their full potential. They are places that focus on the assets of its participants, on possibilities for the future, and on hope.

When all individuals are supported; when people feel comfortable expressing themselves without fear of reprisal; when the focus is on gifts and possibilities each time we gather; when people come together willingly to resolve problems for the common good; when judgment, hierarchies, and winning are vanquished; and when the responsibilities of citizenship are accepted with good hearts, then a degree of success will have been achieved.

This book has presented both the context of the Circle process and the tools for bringing its power to bear in our lives and in our communities. I invite your participation on this journey, as we all work to help families, neighborhoods, communities, and civic and business groups move toward a more peaceful, just, and productive path.

> Never doubt that a small group of thoughtful, committed citizens
> can change the world; indeed, it is the only thing that ever has.[1]

1. Margaret Mead, quoted in Sommers and Dineen, *Curing Nuclear Madness*, 158.

Bibliography

Aggens, Lorenz. "Origins of the Samoan Circle." In *Public Involvement Techniques: A Reader of Ten Years Experience at the Insititute for Water Resources*, prepared by Creighton, Priscoli, et al., 265–70. Institute for Water Resources, US Army Corps of Engineers,1983.

Amstutz, L. S., and Judy H. Mullet. *The Little Book of Restorative Discipline for Schools.* Intercourse, PA: Good Books, 2005.

Auerbach, Jerold S. *Justice without Law?: Resolving Disputes without Lawyers.* New York: Oxford University Press, 1983.

Ball, Jennifer, Wayne Caldwell, and Kay Pranis. *Doing Democracy with Circles: Engaging Communities in Public Planning.* St. Paul, MN: Living Justice, 2010.

Block, Peter. *Community: The Structure of Belonging.* San Francisco: Berrett-Koehler, 2009.

Boggs, Stephen T., and Malcolm Naea Chun. "Ho'oponopono: A Hawaiian Method of Solving Interpersonal Problems." In *Disentangling: Conflict Discourse in Pacific Societies*, edited by Karen Ann Watson-Gegeo and Geoffrey M. White, 122–60. Stanford, CA: Stanford University Press, 1990.

Bopp, Judie. *The Sacred Tree.* 3rd ed. Twin Lakes, WI: Lotus Light, 1989.

Brams, S. J., and Alan D. Taylor. *Fair Division: From Cake-Cutting to Conflict Resolution.* New York: Cambridge University Press, 1996.

Brenneis, Donald. "Dramatic Gestures: The Fiji Indian *Pancayat* as Therapeutic Event." In *Disentangling: Conflict Discourse in Pacific Societies*, edited by Karen Ann Watson-Gegeo and Geoffrrey M. White, 214–38. Stanford, CA: Stanford University Press, 1990.

Carpenter, S. L., and W. J. D. Kennedy. *Managing Public Disputes: A Practical Guide to Handling Conflict and Reaching Agreements.* San Francisco: Jossey-Bass, 1988.

Circle Sentencing: A Yukon Justice Experiment. Produced by Vic Istchenko. Whitehorse, Yukon: Northern Native Broadcasting, 1993. DVD.

Circles. It's About Justice. It's About Healing. Directed by Shanti Thakur, produced by Mark Zannis. Montreal: National Film Board of Canada, 1997. DVD.

Cloke, Ken, and Joan Goldsmith. *Resolving Personal and Organizational Conflict: Stories of Transformation and Forgiveness.* San Francisco: Jossey-Bass, 2000.

Covey, Stephen R. *The 7 Habits of Highly Effective People: Powerful Lessons in Personal Change.* 25th anniversary ed. New York: Simon and Schuster, 2013.

Curry, Andrew. "Gobekli Tepe: The World's First Temple?" *Smithsonian*, November 2008, 1–4.

De Bono, Edward. *Conflicts: A Better Way to Resolve Them.* London: Penguin, 1985.

Duranti, Alessandro. "Doing Things with Words: Conflict, Understanding, and Change in a Samoan Fono." In *Disentangling: Conflict Discourse in Pacific Societies*, edited by Karen Ann Watson-Gegeo and Geoffrey M. White, 459–89. Stanford, CA: Stanford University Press, 1990.

Eagle, Harley. "A Journey in Aboriginal Restorative Justice." *Conciliation Quarterly* 20:3 (2001) 6–8.

Fisher, Roger, and William Ury. *Getting to Yes: Negotiating Agreement without Giving In.* New York: Penguin, 1991.

Frankel, Marvin E. *Partisan Justice.* New York: Hill and Wang, 1980.

Garfield, Charles A., Cindy Spring, and Sedonia Cahill. *Wisdom Circles: A Guide to Self-Discovery and Community Building in Small Groups.* New York: Hyperion, 1998.

Gladwell, Malcolm. *The Tipping Point: How Little Things Can Make a Big Difference.* New York: Little, Brown, 2002.

Goldberg, Marilee C. *The Art of the Question: A Guide to Short-Term Question-Centered Therapy.* New York: Wiley, 1998.

Grunde, Donald A., Jr. *The Iroquois and the Founding of the American Nation.* San Francisco: Indian Historical Press, 1977.

Horgan, John. *The End of War.* San Francisco: McSweeney's, 2012.

Janov, Jill. *The Inventive Organization: Hope and Daring at Work.* San Francisco: Jossey-Bass, 1994.

Kohn, Alfie. *No Contest: The Case against Competition.* New York: Houghton Mifflin, 1992.

Kropotkin, Petr Alekseevich. *Mutual Aid: A Factor of Evolution.* Rev. ed. New York: McClure Phillips, 1904. Online: https://www.forgottenbooks.com/en/books/MutualAid_10074501.

Lavery, Norman G. "Dividing Things Fairly or Fair Divison in the Real World—Part II." ADR Forum. *The Canadian Journal of Dispute Resolution* 13 (July 1997) 4–5.

———. "Mathematics and Mediation?" ADR Forum. *The Canadian Journal of Dispute Resolution* 10 (October 1996) 4–5.

McConnell, Kathryn. "Iroquois Constitution Influenced That of U.S., Historians Say: Smithsonian Editors Interviewed at First Americans Festival." IIP Digital, website of the US Deptartment of State's Bureau of International Information Programs. September 24, 2004. http://iipdigital.usembassy.gov/st/english/article/2004/09/20040924120101akllennoccm9.930056e-02.html#axzz4BKTwpvFR.

McRae, Allan, and Howard Zehr. *The Little Book of Family Group Conferences: New Zealand Style.* Intercourse, PA: Good Books, 2004.

Millar, Margaret. *The Weak-Eyed Bat.* New York: Doubleday, 1942.

More, Hannah. *The Works of Hannah More.* New York: Harper, 1852.

Mozart, Wolfgang Amadeus. *Letters.* Translated by Lady Wallace, edited by Peter Washington and Michael Rose. Everyman's Library. New York: Knopf, 2006.

Nader, L., and Harry F. Todd Jr. "Introduction." In *The Disputing Process: Law in Ten Societies*, edited by Laura Nader and Harry F. Todd Jr., 1–40. New York: Columbia University Press, 1978.

Neihardt, John G. *Black Elk Speaks: Being the Life Story of a Holy Man of the Oglala Sioux.* Albany: State University of New York Press, 2008.

Pranis, Kay. "Building Justice on a Foundation of Democracy, Caring and Mutual Responsibility." Unpublished manuscript. January 2001. Online: http://www.justiceaction.org.au/actNow/Briefs_PDF/WSTRNCRM1.pdf.

————. *The Little Book of Circle Processes: A New/Old Approach to Peacemaking.* Intercourse, PA: Good Books, 2005.

Pranis, Kay, Barry Stuart, and Mark Wedge. *Peacemaking Circles: From Crime to Community.* St. Paul, MN: Living Justice, 2003.

Public Conversations Project training manual. Watertown, MA: 2009.

Pukui, Mary Kawena, E. W. Haertig, and Catherine A. Lee. *Nānā I Ke Kumu (Look to the Source).* Honolulu: Hui Hanai, 1972.

Putnam, R. D., and Lewis M. Feldstein. *Better Together: Restoring the American Community.* New York: Simon and Schuster, 2003.

Quinn, Daniel. *Beyond Civilization: Humanity's Next Great Adventure.* New York: Three Rivers, 1999.

Riestenberg, Nancy. "Restorative Creativity: School Applications of Restorative Processes." *Restorative Justice in Action*, Special School Edition, Spring 2001, 18–19. Online: http://restorativejustice.org/rj-library/restorative-creativity-innovative-school-applications-of-restorative-processes/4174/.

————. "Restorative Schools Grants Final Report: January 2002–June 2003." Unpublished manuscript, 2003. Held by the Minnesota Department of Education, Roseville, MN.

Ross, Rupert. *Dancing with a Ghost: Exploring Indian Reality.* Markham, ON: Reed, 1992.

————. *Returning to the Teachings: Exploring Aboriginal Justice.* Toronto: Penguin, 1996.

Ruffini, Julio L. "Disputing over Livestock in Sardinia." In *The Disputing Process: Law in Ten Societies*, edited by Laura Nader and Harry F. Todd Jr., 209–46. New York: Columbia University Press, 1978.

Sandel, Michael J. *Justice: What's the Right Thing to Do?* New York: Farrar, Straus and Giroux, 2009.

Santayana, George. *The Life of Reason: Or, The Phases of Human Progress.* Vol. 1. New York: Scribner's, 1906.

Sommers, Frank G., and Tana Dineen. *Curing Nuclear Madness.* London: Metheon, 1984.

Stains, Robert R., Jr. "Reflection for Connection: Deepening Dialogue through Reflective Processes." *Conflict Resolution Quarterly* 30:1 (2012) 33–51.

Stiglitz, Joseph E. *The Price of Inequality.* New York: Norton, 2012.

Stuart, Barry. *Building Community Justice Partnerships: Community Peacemaking Circles.* Ottawa, ON: Minister of Justice and the Attorney General of Canada, 1997.

Tannen, Deborah. *The Argument Culture: Stopping America's War on Words.* New York: Ballantine, 1998.

Todd, Harry F., Jr. "Litigious Marginals: Character and Disputing in a Bavarian Village." In *The Disputing Process: Law in Ten Societies*, edited by Laura Nader and Harry F. Todd Jr., 86–121. New York: Columbia University Press, 1978.

12 Angry Men. Directed by Sidney Lumet. 1957. 20th Century Fox, 2007. DVD.

Walker, Lorenn, and Rebecca Greening. *Reentry & Transition Planning Circles for Incarcerated People.* Hawai'i: Hawai'i Friends of Justice & Civic Education, 2011.

Walker, Lorenn, and Leslie A. Hayashi. "Pono Kaulike: A Pilot Restorative Justice Program." *Hawaii Bar Journal*, May 2004, 4–15.

————. "Pono Kaulike: Reducing Violence with Restorative Justice and Solution-Focused Approaches." *Federal Probation* 73:1 (June 2009) 23–27.

Washington State Institute for Public Policy. *Outcome Evaluation of Washington State's Research-Based Programs for Juvenile Offenders.* Doc. no. 04-01-1201. January 2004. Online: http://www.wsipp.wa.gov/Reports/04-01-1201.

Weisstein, Eric W. *CRC Concise Encyclopedia of Mathematics*. 2nd ed. Boca Raton, FL: Chapman & Hall/CRC, 2002.

White, G. M., and Karen Ann Watson-Gegeo. "Disentangling Discourse." In *Disentangling: Conflict Discourse in Pacific Societies*, edited by Karen Ann Watson-Gegeo and Geoffrey M. White, 3–49. Stanford, CA: Stanford University Press, 1990.

Yazzie, Robert. "Traditional Navajo Dispute Resolution in the Navajo Peacemaker Court." *NIDR FORUM*, Spring 1995, 5–16.

Zehr, Howard. *The Little Book of Restorative Justice*. Intercourse, PA: Good Books, 2002.

Zimmer, Carl. "Friends with Benefits." *Time*, February 20, 2012, 3.

Zion, James W. "The Dynamics of Navajo Peacemaking." *Journal of Contemporary Criminal Justice* 14:1 (February,1998) 1–15.